Perceptions of Sense of Community of a Rural Community College

Patricia A. Giero, Ph.D.

Author:	**Patricia Giero, Ph.D.**
Publisher:	**DBC Publishing, Virginia Beach, VA**
Copyright ©	2014; 2016
ISBN Numbers	ISBN-13: 978-0692772867 (DBC Publishing)
	ISBN-10: 0692772863

This text has been altered in format from the original dissertation document to conform to easier to read for the general public and commercial publishing standards. Scholars reviewing the contents and formatting for standardization for thesis or dissertation should *not* use this book's current formatting as a model. Please see your school's guidelines for the acceptable formatting for the graduate level thesis. Alternatively, consult with a professional academic editor for completing your dissertation or publication.

Trademarks:	All brand names, product names, logos, service marks, trademarks or registered trademarks are trademarks of their respective owners.
Cover & Graphics:	Cover Art, Copyright 2016, Dawn D. Boyer, Ph.D. Title Page: Wikimedia Commons, Copyright Free, Public Domain, (Juujuuuujj) Cover: Wikimedia Commons, Hopwas State Park, Copyright Free, Public Domain, (Bs0u10e01)

Disclaimer: The author has attempted to gather as much of the facts and information to the utmost complete and truthfulness for the compilation of this book from bona fide sources, academic databases and libraries, personal interviews, Internet sources, printed material in currently circulating and non-circulating sources, and newspaper articles. Dates noted were from publically and privately available sources. Any data included (left out, incorrectly quoted, or attributed) may be attributed to transcription errors or types. Several bodies of research were interpretations of the same or original documents and errors might have occurred as transcribed. Any reader or researcher with more data to contribute to a future, updated, and corrected version of this project is encouraged to send materials to the researcher's e-mail address noted on this page.

Dr. Giero's research interests are focused on: Adult Education, Criminology and Psychology, Higher Education, Online Learning, Sense of Community, and Sex Offenders.

Follow Dr. Giero on Social Media

LinkedIn profile:	https://www.linkedin.com/in/patriciagiero
Skype:	patricia.giero
Email:	patricia.giero@gmail.com

Perceptions of Sense of Community of a Rural Community College

By

Patricia A Giero, Ph.D.

2012, Doctor of Philosophy, Walden University
2004, Master of Science, Capella University
2000, Bachelor of Arts, University of Maryland University
College

Dissertation Submitted in Partial Fulfillment of the
Requirements for the Degree of

Doctor of Philosophy in Psychology

Walden University, August 2012
College of Social and Behavioral Sciences

This is to certify the doctoral dissertation has been
found to be complete and satisfactory in all
respects, and that any and all revisions required by
the review committee have been made.

Review Committee
Dr. Sandra Harris, Committee Chair, Psychology Faculty
Dr. Arcella Trimble, Committee Member, Psychology Faculty
Dr. Stephen Rice, University Reviewer, Psychology Faculty
Dr. Eric Riedel, Chief Academic Officer

INTRODUCTION

Perceptions of Sense of Community of a Rural Community College

The purpose of this quantitative, non-experimental design study was to investigate sense of community among traditional and non-traditional age students enrolled in online and traditional land-based learning environments. The theoretical foundation for this study was social constructivism, which emphasizes how social interactions impact human growth and development. Previous research has indicated a negative relationship between sense of community and academic and career success. However, there is a gap in the literature regarding sense of community for students in different learning environments of rural community colleges. Specifically, few researchers have examined sense of community of students taking online courses at rural community colleges.

Participants were rural community college students enrolled in 1 of 3 learning environments including online, hybrid, and traditional land-based classes in 2012. The Classroom Community Scale (CCS) was completed by 86 participants. A 2-way ANOVA was used to determine whether student status (traditional versus non-traditional) and type of learning environment (hybrid, online, and traditional land-based courses) impacted the students' sense of community. Results from the study revealed no statistically significant differences between the two groups with regard to sense of community.

Results from the study revealed no statistically significant interaction between student status and type of learning environment. Implications for positive social change includes providing educators information regarding the relationship between sense of community and student retention. This information could be used to encourage course developers and online instructors to create and promote course activities that foster sense of community among students in online courses.

Dedication & Acknowledgements

This dissertation is dedicated to my wonderful children, William, Nathanael, and Nichele. They have traveled with me on this momentous adventure of learning. It has been difficult over the many years. I could not have done this without your patience and support that I needed to 'get it done.' Always and 4ever.

I would like to thank Dr. Sandra Harris, my dissertation chairperson, who guided me through the long and at times arduous process and without whom I am certain I would have not completed this task. Dr. Harris always provided timely and extensive feedback. Even though the 'sea of red' appeared daunting, it provided me the encouragement and necessary information to move to the next paragraph, the next chapter, and to the next revision. Thank you for being there for me, for helping me to learn and grow into 'Dr. Giero,' and for making such a difference in my academic life.

I would also like to thank Dr. Trimble, my dissertation committee member, for your coming on board at the last minute and support in my struggles with committee members and in making this dissertation document something I can be proud of.

I would like to thank Dr. Joyce Hedlund, President of Washington County Community College, and David Markow, Dean of Academic and Student Affairs, for allowing me to conduct my research because without their support this research would not be possible.

I would also like to thank all the students who participated in my research. I know it was a lot to ask during the busy fall semester to find the spare time to respond to my survey. It may have seemed less important than your homework yet you still found the time. I cannot thank you enough for helping me reach this goal.

I would like to thank my family, friends, and all my colleagues for their support and encouragement throughout this journey. Without everyone, this would not have been possible. Words cannot really convey my appreciation ... so, Thank you!

Patricia A. Giero, Ph.D.

Table of Contents

List of Tables

List of Figures

Chapter 1: Introduction to the Study

Background

According to the U. S. Department of Education (USDE, 2004), earning a college degree leads to benefits for the individual and for the society in which the person lives. The primary benefit to the individual is increased income earning potential. According to Hill, Hoffman, and Rex (2005) the earning potential varies according the level of education. Data from the Census Bureau's report, *Current Population Report (CPR)*, which covered the years from 1998-2000, revealed the average yearly income for individuals with a high school diploma was $25,900. The data further showed the average yearly income for college graduates was $45,400 (Day & Newburger, 2002). The report showed individuals who possessed professional degrees such as a Doctor of Medicine (M. D.), Doctor of Jurisprudence (Doctor of Laws) (J. D.), or Doctor of Dental Surgery (D. D. S), earned an average of $99,300 yearly (Day & Newburger, 2002).

Data from the 2007 Census Bureau reported median earnings of $33,000 for high school graduates, $56,000 for college graduates, and $75,000 for those with advanced degrees (Crissey, 2009). Data from the latest Census Bureau (2010) reported (2008) those with a high school diploma earned on average $31,000, those with a bachelor's degree earned about $59,000, and those with an advanced degree earned about $83,000. According to the Bureau of Labor Statistics [BLS, 2010], full-time workers age 25 and over without a high school diploma have an average median weekly earnings of $458, compared with $643 for high school graduates (no college) and $1,141 for those holding at least a bachelor's degree.

Other research has shown the income differential between those with a high school diploma and those having a bachelor's degree has risen from a difference of 38% in the early 1980s to a difference of 92% during the reporting period from 2000 to 2003 for (Hill, Hoffman, & Rex, 2005). According to the U.S. Census Bureau, in 2000, 84% of American adults ages 25 and over, had completed high school and 26% of adults age 25 and older hold a bachelor's degree or higher (Day & Newburger, 2002). In contrast to 1975, 63% of adults had a high school diploma, and 14% had a bachelor's degree (Day & Newburger, 2002). Over the years (1992 to 2009), the number of college-educated people has increased from 27 million to 44 million (BLS, 2010). Having a college degree is not only linked to increased earning potential, the unemployment rate also decreases with each year of education. For example, in 1997 high school graduates had an unemployment rate of 4% while unemployment rate for those with bachelor's degree to doctorate degrees ranged from 1.9% to 1.4% (BLS, 1999).

The economic benefit of a college education extends across a person's life span. The typical college graduate will earn about 73% more of life time income than the average high school graduate (Baum & Payea, 2005). Also, the population of individuals 18 years and over, progressively had higher earnings in 2002 as their level of education increased (Stoops, 2004).

Other research indicates higher education and higher earnings also allows individuals more mobility to change jobs if necessary (Institute for Higher Education Policy, 1998; Moutray, 2009; Theodos & Bednarzik, 2006). Baum and Payea (2005) further indicated educated people are less likely to be unemployed or live in poverty. For example, in 2004, the unemployment rate for white college graduates was 2.8% compared to 4.8% for white high school graduates (Baum & Payea, 2005).

In addition to earning more income over time, research suggests those with higher education engage in healthier behaviors. Higher education is correlated with the decreased prevalence of many health risks (such as cardiovascular risk factors such as diabetes and high blood pressure and cigarette smoking) (Bolen, Rhodes, Powell-Grinner, Bland, & Holtzman, 2000). According to a Gallup poll (Saad, 2002), level of education is among the strongest predictors of whether individuals smoke cigarettes. The Center for Disease Control (2008) reported individuals with General Educational Development (GED) certificates had the highest smoking rate at 41.3%, compared with a rate of less than 6% for individuals with graduate degrees. Research by Baum and Payea (2005) revealed individuals with college degrees have lower smoking rates than those without college degrees. The researchers reported that approximately 33% of individuals without any college education reported they smoke cigarettes compared to 26% of those with some college education. The statistics showed 15% of those with an undergraduate college degree indicated they smoked, and only 10% of those with post-graduate schooling indicated said they smoked (Saad, 2005).

Delpierre, Lauwers-Cances, Datta, Berkman, and Lang (2009) examined the relationship between an individual's social position and health behaviors. More specifically, Delpierre et al. assessed the impact of education levels on healthy behaviors. Using a bivariate analysis of cardiac risk factors such as high blood pressure, blood sugar as it related to diabetes, and cholesterol levels, the findings reported those participants with lower levels of education reported higher levels of risk factors and self-reported they were in poorer health than those with higher levels of education (Delpierre et al., 2009). Delpierre et al. reported among women, those with a lower education level reported higher levels of cardiovascular risk factors than those with higher education. The rate of clinical high blood pressure among women with less than 12 years of education was 39.8%, whereas the rate among women with more than 12 years of education was at 24.6% (Delpierre et al., 2006). Another health issue related to education is prevalence of diabetes. The rate for diabetes among women with less than a high school education was 8.5% and the rate for women with at least a high school education was 4.2%, thus suggesting the more education an individual has received the lower their health risks become.

      The benefits of higher education for society are both monetary and non-monetary (Baum & Payea, 2005; Hill et al., 2005). College educated citizens contribute more to tax revenues at the local, state, and federal levels (Baum & Payea, 2005; Levin, Belfield, Muennig, & Rouse, 2007) than those without college degrees. Male high school dropouts pay approximately $200,000 in taxes over their lifetime; males who graduate from college pay an extra $503,000 - $674,009 in taxes over their lifetime (Levin et al., 2007).

There are also non-monetary benefits for society when citizens have a college degree. As discussed above, educated people are less likely to be unemployed or live in poverty (Baum & Payea, 2005). When people are working, there is less individual dependence for government financial support such as provisions of food stamps, Medicaid, and housing assistance (Baum & Payea, 2005; Institute for Higher Education Policy, 1998). Adults with a college degree are more likely to engage in civic activities such as organized volunteer work, voting, and donating blood (Baum & Payea, 2005). Baum and Payea (2005) reported that 46% of college graduates serve as volunteers in their community compared to 22% for high school graduates. Data from the Bureau of Labor Statistics (2011) revealed that in 2010, 42.3% of college graduates aged 25 years and over, volunteered, compared with 17.9% of high school graduates, and 8% of those with less than a high school diploma.

College educated citizens are also more likely to vote than their non-college educated counterparts. During the 2000 presidential election, 74% of individuals between the ages of 25 and 44 who were college graduates indicated they voted. Conversely only 45% of high school graduates indicated they voted (Baum & Payea, 2005). According to the U. S. Census Bureau's CPR, the voting rate of citizens with at least a bachelor's degree (79%) was higher than those who had not received a high school diploma (39%) (File & Crissey, 2010). Also, voting registration increased in 2008 for those citizens with at least a bachelor's degree at a higher rate (83%) than those who had not received a high school diploma (51%) (File & Crissey, 2010). Baum and Payea (2005) reported that in 1994, 17% of college graduates donated blood on a regular basis, compared to 13% of those with some college, and 11% of high school graduates.

Cumulatively the research shows a college education is important, not only to the individual, but to society as a whole. When individuals successfully complete a college degree the individual increases their earning potential and are more likely to become productive and engaged members of society. As citizens move further into the 21st century, it is imperative more Americans enter into and graduate from college.

The Importance of a College Education

As the United States has transformed from a manufacturing society to a more technology based, global society, having a college education is more important to an individual's personal success than ever before. The BLS has projected almost half of the jobs created by 2018 will require post-secondary education. The BLS (2009) has projected by 2018 the number of occupations that will require a bachelor's degree or higher is expected to be 11.7 million. The BLS further indicates the three fastest growing occupations are computer specialists, network systems analysts, and data communication analysts. The BLS (2009) projects these areas of employment will increase by over 50% as the American society grows more reliant on the Internet. With the growing changes and advances in our society and the world, it is essential for workers to increase their skills and knowledge in order to keep up with the growing trends of our society and the world market. To be competitive in the employment sector, individuals must work toward having a college degree.

Even though there is a documented link between higher wages and having a college degree (Day & Newburger, 2002), it is not easy for everyone to attend college or even to obtain a college degree. Some students may experience difficulties or impediments that prevent them from attending or completing college. For instance, Sherry (1996) pointed out that time constraints, distance, and finances are some factors which impede some individuals from pursuing or completing their educational goals. Many students also face mounting family responsibilities as well as job constraints, both of which may interfere with them going to college (Miller & Lu, 2002). The Internet has become the medium allowing individuals, who might not otherwise have the opportunity, to earn a college degree. Consequently, students are turning to online learning as an alternative to attending traditional classroom based education.

Online Education

The anytime and anywhere availability and format of online courses allows students greater flexibility in gaining access to higher education (Mirakian & Hale, 2007). For instance, for students in rural communities, the distance to the nearest college may be at least 50-100 miles from their home or work. This distance may place such students at a geographical disadvantage when it comes to attending college in the traditional format. Taking classes online may present students in rural areas a viable option for obtaining a college degree. According to several studies (Allen & Seaman, 2007; Kassop, 2003; McGorry, 2003), flexibility in access is one of the main reasons many students take online courses. For institutions to meet the demands for online education, many institutions are offering online courses and programs. Thus many educational institutions offer online courses in order to attract students who would otherwise be outside their traditional service area.

In addition to the flexibility of access, there are other reasons why students turn to online education. Being employed full-time may prevent many students from attending traditional brick-and-mortar (land-based) courses. Thomas (2001) estimated approximately five out of six online students are typically employed and would not be able to attend traditional classes. Economic changes such as higher gas prices have increased the cost associated with attending courses in the traditional land-based format has also made it difficult for some people to go to college. In addition, the decreased revenues associated with the economic downturn have negatively affected the disposable income of many households. These factors have caused potential students to turn to online courses to offset the associated economic costs of going to college (File & Crissey, 2010; Allen & Seaman, 2010b).

The increased demand for online classes has resulted in some institutions offering increased online courses. For instance, three quarters of educational institutions reported an increased demand for new online courses and programs from 2009 to 2010 (Allen & Seaman, 2010a). Allen and Seaman (2010b) conducted a study that revealed more than one in four higher education students take at least one online course. The survey revealed over 4.6 million students took at least one online course during the fall 2008 term. The number of students taking online courses in 2008 was a substantial increase from the 3.5 million students in the fall of 2006 and the 2.3

million students in 2004 (Allen & Seaman, 2003, 2006).

Results from surveys conducted by Allen and Seaman (2003, 2006, 2007 & 2010) and findings from the NCES (1999 & 2008) demonstrated higher education is moving progressively more toward online programs. Results showed the number of higher education institutions offering online courses or degree programs is steadily increasing. NCES (1999) reported use of asynchronous Internet-based technologies grew from 22% of institutions in 1995 to 60% of institutions in 1997-1998. In 2003, 81% of higher education institutions offered at least one fully online or blended course (Allen & Seaman, 2003). In the 2006-2007 academic year, 62-66% of institutions offered some distance educuation course (Allen & Seaman, 2006; NCES, 2008).

Although online classes have increased, affording more individuals the opportunity to obtain college degrees, unlike traditional academic settings, the online environment can lead students to feeling isolated and lonely (Rovai & Wighting, 2005). Research by Hawthornthwaite, Kazmer, Robins, and Shoemaker (2000) has shown feelings of isolation are related to a low sense of community for students in online courses. Some students experience feelings of isolation, and they may eventually drop out of an online course and perhaps drop out of college (Rovai, 2002; Rovai, 2004; Rovai & Wighting, 2005).

A quantitative study by Rovai and Wighting (2005) suggested feelings of isolation can be alleviated when students feel a sense of belonging to a group and when they work together in a community. For instance, when students discuss their educational values, goals, and expectations they may feel an increased sense of connectedness to others in the class (Rovai & Wighting, 2005). In turn, the sense of connectedness may promote a sense of community for students and the sense of community may promote higher achievement and persistence in the course. Students who have a greater sense of community are more likely to persevere in their courses than those who feel alienated and alone (Tinto, 1993). Also, according to Rovai (2002b), online learners that have a strong sense of community and are less likely to feel isolated. Those students also "have greater satisfaction with their academic programs" (p. 328).

The focus of this research was to explore students' perception of sense of community various learning environments within a rural community college. This information could be used to explain how sense of community may be fostered in the virtual environment. The information could also be used to make practical recommendations to online instructors and to course designers to incorporate activities that promote a sense of community in online classes so that students have the opportunity to have a positive learning experience. The research question which guided this study was "how does sense of community vary for traditional versus non-traditional students taking online, hybrid, and traditional land-based courses at a rural community college?"

Sense of Community

Sense of community is defined as "a feeling that members have of belonging, feeling that members matter to one another and to the group, and a shared faith that members' needs will be met through their commitment to be together" (McMillan & Chavis, 1986, p. 9). Sense of community plays a distinct role in students' success in their courses and in college. For instance, sense of community contributes to students' overall learning experience by increasing motivation, increasing learning, and decreasing feelings of isolation (Boston, Diaz, Gibson, Ice, Richardson, & Swan, 2009; Shen, Nuankhieo, Amelung, & Laffey, 2008; Wighting, Liu, & Rovai, 2008).

Motivation is an important aspect in learning. According to Wighting, Liu, and Rovai (2002) and Ryan and Deci (2000), students with higher motivation, in particular intrinsic motivation, tend to achieve more and have a greater curiosity for learning. Intrinsic motivation can be defined as "doing an activity for its inherent satisfactions rather than for fro some separable consequence" (Ryan & Deci, 2000, p. 56).

Sense of community plays a significant role in promoting a successful learning experience for students (Dawson, 2008; Liu, Magjuka, Bonk, & Lee, 2007; Rovai, 2002; Rovai & Jordan, 2004). According to Rovai (2002), connectedness is the first component of sense of community. It is the feeling of belongingness and acceptance and leads to the creation of bonding relationships. Learning is the second component of classroom community. In a classroom community, learning is the feeling that knowledge and meaning are actively constructed. It is the component of the learning community that helps students develop knowledge of, and the understanding of course material, through interaction among its members (Rovai, 2002b). Hence, a classroom community can be "viewed as a social community of learners who share knowledge, values, and goals." (Rovai, 2002, p. 322)

When students contribute to a sense of community by sharing their goals and values, those students are less likely to experience feelings of loneliness and isolation (Rovai, 2002; Rovai & Jordan, 2004). Rovai and Wighting (2005) examined sense of community and feelings of alienation among online students. The findings indicated a student's sense of alienation and isolation was inversely related to the student's sense of community. Participants with both strong feelings of social isolation and powerlessness were also likely to have a weaker sense of connectedness and learning (Rovai & Wighting, 2005). Rovai and Wighting's (2005) study highlighted the importance of reducing a student's sense of alienation and isolation in an online course. Research by Rovai (2001) suggested that interaction is one important element for reducing feelings of isolation.

As suggested by Rovai (2001), interaction is important not only in learning but also in promoting a sense of positive outcomes in the classroom. Several quantitative studies (Adbous & Yen, 2010; Bollinger & Martindale, 2004) indicated that course room interaction is related to positive student learning outcomes and student satisfaction. Palmer and Holt (2008) conducted research which revealed a positive correlation between learner satisfaction and learning outcomes in the online environment. Factors that positively influenced student satisfaction were the students' confidence level about their ability to communicate and learn online; students having a clear understanding of the requirements of the class; knowing what was needed in order to succeed in the class with a good grade; and how well the students' thought they were performing in the class (Palmer & Holt, 2008; Sun, Tsai, Finger, Chen, & Yeh, 2008). When students are satisfied with the learning experience they are more likely to complete their online courses (and subsequently their college degree (Palloff & Pratt, 2007; Rovai & Wighting, 2005).

When students engage each other and learn together in a community, they are able to share their ideas and experiences. It is this interaction or social interaction that is a key ingredient in building a sense of community (Lock, 2002; Palloff & Pratt, 2007; Swan, 2007). Research has demonstrated that interaction is a key element in fostering sense of community in an online environment (Dawson, 2006; Rovai, 2002b; Swan, 2002).

Rovai and Wighting (2005) conducted a quantitative study that found a relationship between sense of community and a sense of feeling alienated in a virtual classroom. Sense of community was broken into sub-components of connectedness and learning. Feelings of alienation were broken into the three components of social isolation, powerlessness, and normlessness. The results revealed inverse relationships between sense of community and feelings of alienation. The data revealed the higher the student's sense of community, the weaker the student's sense of isolation and alienation in the classroom. Participants with strong feelings of social isolation and powerlessness were likely to have a weaker sense of connectedness and learning (Rovai & Wighting,

2005). To decrease the likelihood students might experience feelings of loneliness and isolation, the online learning environment must promote interaction and collaboration among learners. Interaction among the members in the online class plays a significant role in a student having a successful learning experience (Dawson, 2006, 2008; Liu, Magjuka, Bonk, & Lee, 2007; Rovai, 2002; Rovai & Jordan, 2004).

Arbaugh and Benbunan-Fich (2007) sampled 40 online MBA courses to determine whether learner–instructor, learner–learner, or learner–system interaction was most significantly related to online course outcomes. The findings revealed that collaborative environments were associated with higher levels of learner–learner and learner–system interaction. The learner–instructor and learner–system interaction was significantly and positively associated with students' perceived level of learning (Arbaugh & Benbunan-Fich, 2006). Arbaugh and Benbunan-Fich's findings also suggested as students engaged in more discussions with other students and the course instructor, their overall satisfaction with the course increased and their overall satisfaction with the online environment improved.

When students interact and participate in online discussions by exchanging ideas and experiences, the interaction encourages a sense of connection among students and fosters a sense of community. Kala et al. (2010) suggested using electronic technology can be used to enhance active learning and support collaborative learning. These technologies include blogs, e-mail, discussion boards, and video streaming. Each type of technology can allow the learner to collaborate on activities and share resources. The interaction and processing of knowledge by the students will help foster sense of community. When there is a strong sense of community, the student is more likely to complete their courses. Positive sense of community is also related to improved learning outcomes for students. For example, Benbunan-Fich and Arbaugh (2006) pointed out when students are engaged in collaborative assignments students earn, on average, better grades in courses. Cumulatively research shows that encouraging and fostering positive social interactions and promotes active learning and enhances the students' sense of community (Rovai, 2007).

Demographic Variables that May Affect Sense of Community in the Online Environment

Dziuban, Moskal, and Hartman (2005) reported today's college students are more diverse. The student population for most community colleges usually consists of non-traditional, low-income, and minority students (Provasnik & Planty, 2008). Researchers (Benshoff &

Lewis, 1992; Cross, 1980; Hemby, 1998) define a non-traditional student as an adult who returns to school full- or part-time while maintaining responsibilities such as employment, family, and other responsibilities of adult life. The group of non-traditional college students tend to have responsibilities of both work and family so their demands, and challenges, may be greater than those of someone younger.

Non-traditional and Traditional Students

The student population for most community colleges is usually non-traditional, low-income, and minority students (Provasnik & Planty, 2008). According to the National Institute of Education Statistics, nearly 75% of all undergraduate students in both 4-year and two-year postsecondary institutions are in some way non-traditional (IES, 2009). Researchers (Benshoff & Lewis, 1992; Cross, 1980; Hemby, 1998) define a non-traditional student as an adult who returns to school full- or part-time and maintaining responsibilities such as employment, family, and other responsibilities of adult life. Traditional students are those that are between the ages of 18 and 25 and attend college immediately following high school. According to the U.S. Department of Education's National Center for Education Statistics (2002), traditional students are viewed as dependents who fall between the ages of 18 and 23.

There are other factors which are related to being a non-traditional student. Those factors include being a single parent, being divorced, the presence of younger children, and low-income status (Taniguchi & Kaufman, 2007). Being a single parent is one factor in becoming a non-traditional student. Non-traditional enrollment may be a way to improve or compensate for the loss of marital resources by becoming more marketable by means of education. In 2010, the BLS (2011c), women were employed in 67% of families with no spouse present.

Older students with children have many financial barriers that may interfere with their ability to pursue take traditional classroom based courses. According to the U. S. Department of Agriculture (Lino, 2011), the annual child-rearing expense estimates ranged between $11,880 and $13,830 for a child in a two-child, married-couple family in the middle-income group. The average range for full-time children for an infant in a childcare center is $4,650 – $18,200 (National Association of Child Care Resource & Referral Agencies, 2011). These costs, in addition to college tuition (approximately $24,483 annually for a 2-year institution and $32,790 for a 4-year institution (NCES, 2011), may put a financial strain on students seeking higher education. The expected costs of raising children may motivate parents to seek educational opportunities to enable them to provide for their family. These non-traditional students may see online courses as a way of increasing their earning potential.

Older students may experience more technological challenges in the online environment than their younger counterparts. When contemporary technologies such as software associated with online learning are integrated into the educational environment, the lack of familiarity from older, non-traditional students may create barriers to learning (Tanner, 2007). As new technology emerges in both the workforce and in educational settings it requires the learning of new and different skills. It is this influx of technology into these settings that may negatively impact the learning of older students. Older adults may be less likely than younger adults to have familiarity with and experience with the new technology (Czaja & Sharit, 1993; Gatto & Tak, 2008).

Generational differences may also impact student performance in online courses. The Baby Boomers (individuals who were born between the years 1943 and 1960) may prefer the using the telephone to using the cellular phone (Rodriguez, Green, & Ree, 2003). Traditional age students tend to have more technologically savvy and are more likely to have computers in their homes than non-traditional age students. Younger students, typically those from Generation X (individuals who were born between the years 1960 and 1980), were born during the explosion of technology. These students have had access to computers from an early age. Students from Generation X tend to be more comfortable with using technology and may be more proficient at surfing the Internet and communicating through e-mail, beepers, and cellular phones.

Non-traditional students may have difficulty experiencing sense of community with their younger counterparts. A lack of interaction or miscommunication in an online course, may create some barriers for the non-traditional student. For example, a difference of opinion between students in online course may be misconstrued as a verbal attack (Epp, Green, Rahman, & Weaver, 2010). The older non-traditional student may not feel as connected to their classmates. This sense of being disconnected from their classmates may cause the non-traditional to feel he or she is not a member of the learning community (Rovai, Wighting, & Jing, 2005).

Problem Statement

Individuals seeking a college education have several options available to them. Students can attend online courses, participate in other distance learning options, or participate in a campus education. The increased demand for online classes has resulted in some institutions offering more online courses. For instance, three quarters of educational institutions reported an increased demand for new online courses and programs from 2009 to 2010 (Allen & Seaman, 2010a). One study (Allen & Seaman, 2010b) used survey research to reveal more than one in four higher education students take at least one online course. The survey further revealed that over 4.6 million students took at least one online course during the fall 2008 term.

Previous research has shown students who have a difficult time in a course withdraw at a higher rate for an online course versus students in a blended (or traditional) classroom course format (Dzuiban, Hartman, & Moskal, 2004; Pigliapoco & Bogliolo, 2007; Rovai, 2003; Willging & Johnson, 2004). Students who do not feel a sense of community in online learning environments tend to feel isolated and lonely; subsequently there is the potential for failure in the classroom and in their overall educational goals (Rovai & Wighting, 2005). This failure may turn put the students at risk for dropping out of school.

Other research shows student attrition has the potential to rise when students are unable to experience a sense of community in online classes (Rovai & Wighting, 2005). Research suggests students who do not develop a sense of community do not make connections to the course content or to other students in the class (Haythornthwaite,

Kazmer, Robins, & Shoemaker, 2000: Pigliapoco & Bogliolo, 2007). When students do not make connections with the fellow classmates, they may feel isolated and lonely (Pigliapoco & Bogliolo, 2007; Rovai & Jordan, 2004).

There is some limited research conducted that examines the sense of community by learning environment of community college students in rural areas. Specifically, few researchers have examined the sense of community of students taking online courses at rural community colleges.

Purpose of Study

The purpose of this quantitative, non-experimental study was to examine student perceptions of sense of community in a community college located in New England. The researcher used a survey methodology to collect data that allowed examination of sense of community among traditional and non-traditional students enrolled in online and traditional land-based learning environments at two rural community colleges. The study included data from students who are currently enrolled in undergraduate degree-based programs. The dependent variable was sense of community as reflected by scores on the CCS. The independent variables were student status (traditional or non-traditional) and learning environment (online and traditional land-based courses). Traditional students were defined as students between 18 and 23 years of age (NCES, 2002). Non-traditional students were defined as students 24 years old or older. Demographic data such as age, ethnicity, gender, number of children, and income level, employment status (full-time or part-time), number of hours worked, and number of online and hybrid courses taken were also collected. These demographic variables were used to describe the overall sample to determine if the sample is representative of the larger population of community college students. The representativeness of the sample impacted the generalizability of the results from the study. A demographic questionnaire was provided. Additional information regarding the variables is located in chapters 2 and 3.

Nature of the Study

This non-experimental, quantitative study used a survey methodology to explore differences between sense of community among traditional and non-traditional students enrolled in online and traditional land-based learning environments at two rural community colleges. The variables were not manipulated, there was no control or comparison group, and there was no random assignment of participant to groups, (Gravetter & Wallnau, 2007; Trochim, 2006). In addition, non-experimental designs are frequently used in research to describe current existing characteristics such as attitudes, perceptions, values, etc. (Trochim, 2006). Therefore, the study was a non-experimental design. The research question which guided this study was, "how does sense of community vary for traditional versus non-traditional students taking online, hybrid, and traditional land-based courses at a rural community college?"

Surveys were used to collect data from undergraduate students enrolled in a degree program from a rural community college. Sense of community was assessed using the Classroom Community Scale (CCS) (Rovai, 2002a). The dependent variable was sense of community as reflected by scores on the CCS. The independent variables were student status (traditional or non-traditional) and the type of learning environment (online, hybrid, and traditional land-based courses).

Demographic data such as age, ethnicity, gender, number of children, and income level, employment status (full-time or part-time), number of hours worked, and number of online and hybrid courses were taken to further describe the overall sample to see if it affects the largest sample of community college students. There were a number of factors that characteristically separate non-traditional students from traditional students (Benshoff & Lewis, 1992). The demographics further described the overall sample of community college students. A demographic questionnaire was provided. The population for this study consisted of students enrolled in a degree-based community college degree program who were over the age of 18.

Participants were recruited and contacted via the community college e-mail system. The presidents of the colleges were contacted to gain permission to conduct the research (see Appendix A). The sample consisted of a minimum of 21 participants for each of the two learning environment (traditional-land-based and online) for an overall total sample size of a minimum of 63 participants. This sample size was based on a power analysis using Cohen's d (1992). The general accepted value for power is .80 (80%), with a medium effect size of .14. A purposive sampling method was used to recruit participants for the study. Additional information regarding the sampling procedures is located in chapter 3.

Students were e-mailed an invitation letter (see Appendix B) with a link to the web-based version of the CCS. As an adjunct faculty member of the community college, I had access to the college e-mail system and e-mail accounts. Prior to conducting any research, IRB Approval was required as well as permission from the community colleges. Also, directions were provided in the initial recruitment e-mail regarding directions to accessing the survey online. Participants completed the CCS, demographic questions, and a consent form on the confidential website Survey Monkey (www. surveymonkey. com). The URL link to the survey tool was provided in the initial e-mail that invited students to participate in the study. Participants were encouraged to print a copy of the consent form for their records. The CCS was the primary tool for collecting data for this study. The CCS is a valid psychometric assessment tool for examining sense of community. The CCS has been used in previous research with consistent empirical results over time. Additional information regarding the reliability and validity of the instrument is located in chapter 3.

Research Questions/Hypotheses

The general research question which guided this study was, "how does traditional versus non-traditional students at a rural community college compare in their sense of community?" Students were classified as traditional or non-traditional status according to age. The research is guided by the following research questions:

1. What is the difference in overall perceived sense of community for students taking online and traditional land-based courses?

H_O: There is no statistically significant difference in overall perceived sense of community, as measured by the CCS, for community college students taking online and traditional land-based courses.

H_A: There is a statistically significant difference in overall perceived sense of community, as measured by the CCS, for community college students taking online and traditional land-based courses.

2. How does being either a traditional student versus a non-traditional student affect sense of community between traditional and non-traditional students in a rural community college?

H_O: There is no statistically significant difference in overall perceived sense of community, as measured by the CCS, between traditional and non-traditional age students.

H_A: There is a statistically significant difference in overall perceived sense of community, as measured by the CCS, between traditional and non-traditional age students.

3. How does student status (traditional versus non-traditional) and type of learning environment (online and traditional land based) interact to impact the sense of community for students in a rural community college?

H_O: Student status (traditional versus non-traditional) and type of learning environment (online and traditional land based) do not interact to produce a statistically significant difference in the sense of community for students in a rural community college. H_A: Student status (traditional versus non-traditional) and type of learning environment (online and traditional land based) do interact to produce a statistically significant difference in the sense of community for students in a rural community college.

Data Collection and Analysis

The CCS was the primary tool for collecting data for this study. The CCS is a valid psychometric assessment tool for examining sense of community. The CCS has been used in previous research with consistent empirical results over time by measuring the same constructs of community, connectedness, and learning. Additional information regarding the reliability and validity of the instrument is located in chapter 3.

The null hypothesis for the research questions were tested using the two-way analysis of variance (ANOVA) procedure. A two-way ANOVA is used when there are two independent variables and one dependent variable (Huck, 2008). A two-way ANOVA allows researchers to compare the effect of multiple levels of two independent variables. A two-way ANOVA will evaluate the interaction between the two independent variables (student status and learning environments). The statistical assumptions for the two-way ANOVA was checked before the two-way ANOVA is conducted to see if the assumptions were upheld for the participants in the study. It is important to test for assumptions first. When the assumptions of a test are satisfied, the researcher can be confident the test has produced a justified conclusion (Gravetter & Wallnau, 2007). Different statistical tests have different assumptions about the distribution of the data for the variables being sampled in the study. The assumptions that were tested include interval scale of measurement for the dependent variable, independence, normality, and homogeneity of variance (Howell, 2004). Additional details of how the assumptions were tested are presented in chapter 3. The researcher was cognizant of the fundamental conditions associated with each type of statistical test to ensure the test was used appropriately. Additional information regarding the data collection and analysis is located in chapter 3.

Theoretical Foundation

The theoretical foundation for this study was social constructivism, which emphasizes how social interactions with others enhance the learning process. Research shows optimal learning occurs in a constructivist setting (Jonassen, Peck, & Wilson, 1999; Kasworm, 2003; Vygostky, 1978). Humans are social creatures. They tend to grow and develop through social interactions in a variety of communities (Woo & Reeves, 2007). According to Vygotsky (1978), cognitive functions are viewed as products of interactions of others. The types of interactions in a classroom include discussion with other students, interactions with the teacher, etc. Learning is primarily a social process. Students' conversations with classmates allow haring of backgrounds; and to participate in give and take of collaborative, cooperative activities (Sthaporn-nanon, Sakulbumrungsil, Theeraroungchaisri & Watch-aradamrongkun, 2009). Woo and Reeves (2007) admitted not all conversations and discussions result in meaningful learning. Meaningful interaction consists of sharing and responding to ideas. It is negotiating both internally and socially among the class members. It also permits one to defend one's ideas and to offer alternative perspectives with one another while engaging in relevant collaborative activities (Vygotsky, 1978; Woo & Reeves, 2007).

The theory of social constructivism has primarily been used for the traditional classroom. However, as online classrooms begin to develop and grow, the principles of constructivism can also be used to explain how sense of community is developed in online and hybrid courses. Redfern and Naughton (2002) stated learning is not achieved as an "isolated individual act, but a collective result of social interaction" (p. 2). In order for this social interaction to occur and learning to occur, a sense of community must be built (Redfern & Naughton, 2002; Rovai & Wighting, 2005; Shea, 2006).

Social constructivism is a philosophy of learning based on how knowledge is constructed by the individual through interaction with the environment (Huang, 2002; Rovai, 2004). Constructivism was influenced by Dewey (1916), Piaget (1973) and Vygotsky (1978). Dewey (1916), proposed knowledge is gained from an individual's experience from the environment. Dewey believed the teacher was a guide through interaction. Teachers are not only the main communicators of knowledge and skills but guide the students into a role of creating their own knowledge (Dewey, 1938). Meaning and knowledge construction is achieved by making connections with other things and other individuals through the process of interaction. Both Piaget and Dewey believed the teacher helped shape the individual's real experiences through interactions with the environment (Huang, 2002; Ornstein & Hunkins, 1998).

Vygostky focused on the effects of social interaction, language, and culture on learning (Vygotsky, 1978; Woo & Reeves, 2007). Vygotsky believed psychological development and instruction is achieved and embedded on a social plane through dialogue (Vygotsky, 1978). Vygotsky (1978) proposed that meaning is constructed through the process of sharing of perspectives and experiences through collaborative relationship (Rovai & Wighting, 2005; Woo & Reeves, 2007).

Vygotsky's (1978) conception of social constructivism provides the foundation for the proposed study. Vygotsky (1978) believed "human learning pre-supposes a specific social nature" (p. 88), and he emphasized students do not learn in isolation, but rather through collaboration within social environments. The collaboration and interaction between both students and instructors enables students to perceive they are part of a shared learning community. Students who feel isolated and alienated in their courses due to lack of interaction with their teachers and other students may lack a sense of classroom community (Rovai & Wighting, 2005).

Learning is a result of active social interaction among learners (Rovai & Wighting, 2005). Learning is achieved when there is a strong sense of community among its members (Rovai & Wighting, 2005). For this reason, educators and instructional designers need to develop collaborative activities and online instructional strategies that foster this social interaction and promote a strong sense of community among the students. Student-to-student as well as instructor-to-student interaction will help reduce feelings of isolation and promote high achievement among all students (Rovai & Wighting, 2005).

Definition of Terms

The research on sense of community and online education utilizes some operational terms. Those terms are defined for the purpose of the study as follows:

Asynchronous learning. Learning that is independent of time or place. Participants can engage class activities and discussions at individually determined times (Hrastinski, 2008).

Blended learning environment. A learning environment that combines face-to-face instructions with technology-mediated instruction (Rovai & Jordan, 2004).

Community. A group of individuals with shared emotional connection. Members of the group have a feeling that each matter to one another and to the group and have a shared trust that members' needs will be met through their commitment of working together (McMillan & Chavis, 1986).

Hybrid model of instruction. Instruction is combined with traditional face-to-face and online learning so instruction occurs both in the classroom and online (Rovai & Jordan, 2004). Alternative term for blended learning environment.

Learning community. A group of students in a learning community whereby the students have a strong emotional connection and a sense of belonging. The students are committed to their shared educational goals (Rovai, 2002a, 2002c; Rovai & Ponton, 2005; Outzs, 2006, p. 286)

Non-traditional students. A student who is aged 24 years or older (NCES, 2002).

Online instruction. Instruction where most or all of the course content is delivered online. A type of instruction that typically does not have any face-to-face interaction (Rovai & Jordan, 2004).

Sense of Community. A feeling of connectedness and sense of belonging members share along with group norms and values and the extent to which their educational goals and expectations are satisfied by group membership (Rovai, 2002c).

Traditional students. A student based on the ages between 18 and 23 (NCES, 2002).

Traditional Face-to-Face Instruction. Face-to-face instruction that includes courses in which the majority of instruction is delivered on campus for a specified amount of time. The students generally reside in the same geographic area (Allen & Seaman, 2010).

Assumptions of the Study

There are several assumptions related to this study. First, the study was founded in the assumption the CCS is a psychometrically sound assessment tool for assessing students' sense of community. Psychometric properties are important in the construction and validation of measurement instruments such as the CCS. Research has shown the CCS is a psychometrically sound instrument. Details regarding the psychometric properties of the instrument are presented in Chapter 3).

Second, the instrument used was appropriate for the sample. The researcher assumed students enrolled at a community college in any of the three learning environments: online, blended, or traditional land-based; were capable of understanding and completing the CCS accurately. The researcher assumed participants were willing to participate in the study, and they would respond to the survey questions honestly.

Third, in order for a study to be valid, the participants were representatives of the population of interest to the study. For example, the participants would not behave differently than they would were they not participating in this research study. Validity represents whether an instrument measures what it intends (Gravetter & Wallnau, 2007). The external validity of this study assumed the findings of this study were generalizable to other institutions and courses. The internal validity assumed the non-experimental, quantitative study using a survey methodology was a way to gather the information to explore differences between sense of community among traditional and non-traditional students enrolled in online, hybrid, and traditional land-based learning environments at a rural community college (Trochim, 2006).

Finally, the researcher also assumed assumptions for the statistical analysis, the two-way ANOVA would be met. The validity of the results was predicated upon the degree to which the assumptions of the statistical procedure, the two-way ANOVA were met. Details regarding the and the procedures for testing the assumptions will be addressed in chapter 3.

Limitations of the Study

In conducting this study, the following limitations were taken into account. The study population was limited to undergraduate students enrolled at two sites. This sample may not be generalized to other institutions and courses, thus limiting generalizability and external validity of the findings (Trochim, 2006). The sample was taken from two rural community college and may not be generalizable to larger, more urban, community colleges. For example, Washington County, the county in which the college is located in has a population of 32,856 for 2010. In contrast, a southern area in which a community college exists, Cumberland County, has a population of 281,674 for 2010 (U. S. Census Bureau, 2011). The findings of this study may not be generalized outside those who will participate.

This study focused on undergraduate college students; therefore, the results may or may not be generalizable to graduate students with a higher educational level. Since this study did not use a random sampling of students, this may decrease the generalizability of the findings to other populations of community college students. The sampling frame has defined the target population as those enrolled at the community colleges from which the sample was drawn and to which the sample data was generalized. For this study, a purposive sampling method was used. According to Robson (2002) a purposive sample is used when "the researcher has to achieve a particular purpose" (p. 264). For the purpose of this study, the purposive sample was required to measure classroom community among students in two learning environments. Therefore, results only reflect the population of undergraduate community college students from which the data was collected.

Some other confounding variables that could potentially have impacted the students' perception of sense of community included instructor teaching style, teaching philosophy, and online experience of the teacher. For example, when teachers initiate dialogue and illustrate course concepts through activities that build essential skills and knowledge for the students it clarifies concepts and reduces students' confusion (Tsai, 2007). When the teacher lacks the skills to facilitate and moderate online discussions, this limits the opportunities for collaboration and interaction among the students (Rovai & Downey, 2010). As a result, this may have limited the opportunities for students to establish sense of community in online classes. Some variables not included in the study were teaching style, teaching philosophy, and online experience of the teacher. There may be fundamental differences in instructional strategies of the course of the teachers, which may have impacted the class' sense of community.

Significance of Study

This study investigated whether there is a difference in sense of community for traditional and non-traditional students taking online and traditional land-based courses. The findings from this non-experimental quantitative research may benefit not only academic institutions but the students in online courses. Specifically, the information may benefit students through learning what perceptions others students have that fostered a learning community. Rovai (2002c) acknowledged to increase retention of students, faculty and educational institutions must provide increased support by promoting a strong sense of community. This can be accomplished through establishing strategies that enable students to establish and make connections with other learners. Sense of community can also be fostered through actions that provide students with a large base of academic support (Rovai, 2002c).

The information gained from the survey helped the

community colleges gain a better understanding as to the degree to which the different learning environments foster sense of community for its students. By examining the various learning environments (traditional land-based and online), institutions can gain a better understanding of which learning environment has the potential to foster a sense of community. Communities are built through interaction from both the student and the teacher (Rovai, 2001; Rovai & Wighting, 2005; Swan, 2002). This interaction can be accomplished through innovative course design and enhanced collaborative and facilitative online instructional strategies (Rovai & Wighting, 2005). This researh helped achieve these aims through an understanding of the students' perceptions of sense of community.

The current literature with regard to sense of community in an online learning environment indicated sense of community is fostered through interaction and collaboration among the learners. It is this interaction and collaboration that plays a significant role in promoting a successful learning experience for students (Dawson, 2008; Liu, Magjuka, Bonk, & Lee, 2007; Rovai, 2002; Rovai & Jordan, 2004). The number of online courses for both 2- and 4-year institutions is growing. There is minimal evidence that explored how sense of community among rural community college students impact student performance. To address the gap in literature this research study examined how the students in an undergraduate online and traditional land-based learning environment perceive sense of community. The researcher also explored the relationship between age and sense of community.

As rural community colleges expand their online courses and curriculum to meet the growing needs of the community, they are trying to catch up on the growing trends of online education. The knowledge gained from this study aided in this task. The colleges could use the results of my study to help the needs of the students in online courses.

Practical Implications

The findings from this research have implications for continued research on sense of community and how it impacts student retention and performance. Future research might examine the relationship between teaching style, teaching philosophy, and sense of community among students in online courses. There may be fundamental differences in instructional strategies of the online course instructors, which may impact the students' sense of community in online course.

This information was also used to explain how sense of community may be fostered in the virtual environment. The information could also be used to make practical recommendations to online instructors and to course designers to incorporate activities that promote a sense of community in online classes so students have the opportunity for a positive learning experience. Specifically, this knowledge gained from this research provided information about whether the online and face-to-face courses differ in terms of how they affect student's sense of community. This information may be the catalyst for having discussions to determine how the course activities differ and which activities might be most effective in promoting sense of community.

The implication for positive social change included assisting rural community colleges in decreasing attrition and promoting retention in online courses. This study did shed some light on the perceptions of the students as to what does or does not foster sense of community using an online survey. Community colleges can increase student retention by providing increased support by promoting a strong sense of community (Rovai, 2002c). This can be accomplished through establishing strategies online to establish and make those connections through active communication, meaningful interactions, and participation (Misanchuk & Anderson, 2001; Stepich & Ertmer, 2003; Tu

& Corry, 2001) with other learners as well as providing students with a larger base of academic support (Rovai, 2002c). This study assisted in providing necessary information from the students' perception on what would or would not foster sense of community to decrease attrition and promote retention in online courses.

Summary

From the research of sense of community, it appeared that sense of community does impacts student attrition and retention. Previous research has shown students who have a difficult time in a course withdrew at a higher rate for an online course section than those in a blended course or traditional classroom format of the course (Dzuiban, Hartman, &Moskal, 2004; Pigliapoco & Bogliolo, 2007; Rovai, 2003; Willging & Johnson, 2004). Students who feel a lack of community in online learning environments tend to feel isolated and lonely; there is the potential for failure in the classroom and in their overall goals for education (Rovai & Wighting, 2005). This failure in turns puts the students at risk for dropping out of school (Rovai & Jordan, 2004).

As the United States has transformed from a manufacturing society to a more technology-based global society, having a college education is more important to an individual's personal success than ever before. The BLS (2009) has projected by 2018 the number of occupations requiring a bachelor's degree or higher is expected to be 11.7 million. The research shows a college education is important not only to the individual but to society as a whole (USDE, 2004). When individuals successfully complete a college degree the individual increases their earning potential and are more likely to become productive and engaged members of society.

Educational institutions are jumping on this projection of the importance of having a college education. Students can attend online courses, participate in other distance learning options, or participate in a campus education. The increased demand for online classes has resulted in some institutions offering more online courses. For instance, three quarters of educational institutions reported an increased demand for new online courses and programs from 2009 to 2010 (Allen & Seaman, 2010a).

Some of those challenges to getting a college degree are time constraints, distance, and finances (Sherry, 2006). Many students face mounting family responsibilities and job constraints. Online education has allowed many individuals minimize some of these challenges and have an opportunity to obtain a college degree. By understanding how sense of community impacts student success in an online course, community colleges can develop and design online courses that will meet the needs of its community members.

Chapter 2 focuses on the theoretical framework that is the foundation of the study and the literature related to sense of community and online learning environments. The variables and research methods for this study are also be discussed. Chapter 2 provides an examination on the advantages and disadvantages to online courses.

Chapter 3 focuses on the methodology of the research to include a discussion of how the research was conducted and analyzed in the examination of sense of community and online courses and if age was significant in developing sense of community. Chapter 4 contains the data analysis and the results of the study. The chapter provides a detailed description of the participants. The chapter also provides a detailed discussion on the results utilizing the appropriate statistical procedures that examined each of the hypotheses. Finally, chapter 5 comprises a discussion of the results of the study and the impact of age on sense of community as it relates to online courses, in addition, the implications on how this research can facilitate social change and recommendations for future research.

Chapter 2: Literature Review

Organization, Strategy, and Justification of the Study

Organization of the Review

The purpose of this quantitative, non-experimental study was to investigate the differences between in sense of community for traditional and non-traditional age undergraduate students in online and traditional courses. The research question guiding this study was "To what degree does being a traditional student versus a non-traditional impacts students' sense of community?" This chapter will provide an in-depth analysis of the literature regarding sense of community. The first section discusses the theoretical foundation utilized in the study. The specific theory used for this study is social constructivism. The second section discusses the growing trends in online education in institutions in higher education and the benefits of online education. The third section introduces the literature regarding sense of community in higher education, the components of sense of community, and the advantages and disadvantages of sense of community for students pursuing online studies. The fourth section explores the link between sense of community and student learning outcomes. The fifth section discusses sense of community and the level of inteaction between the teacher and the student as well as between studentsand their fellow classmates. Research has shown interaction is crucial to students success in online learning (Rovai, 2001; Swan, 2002, 2003; Webb-Boyd, 2008; Woo & Reeves, 2007). The sixth section presents the Classroom Community Scale (Rovai, 2002) and how it has been used in past research to examine individual perceptions of sense of community in a given classroom or context. The chapter concludes with a summary of the literature review.

Strategies for Searching the Literature

The review of literature for this study was accomplished primarily by searching online research databases and government websites. The research databases utilized included Academic Search Premier, Education Resources Information Center (ERIC), ProQuest, and Science Direct. The key words and phrases used to identity relevant literature consisted of the following: *evaluation of online learning courses in higher education, adult learning theory, relationship between social networks and a sense of community, student differences in online and blended learning environments, and social extent of asynchronous learning.*

Sense of Community

The concept of sense of community was pioneered by Sarason (1974) who defined sense of community as "the perception of similarity to others, an acknowledgement inter-dependence by giving to or doing for others what one expects from them ... the feeling that one is part of a larger dependable and stable structure" (p. 157). This definition posits that sense of community is promoted through socializaton, which is a social process through which students interact through their presence in the learning environment (McMillan & Chavis, 1986; Outzs, 2006; Rovai, 2002c; Rovai & Lucking, 2003). Social process is seen as when students' learn values, beliefs, culture, and knowledge during the shared interaction in the online learning environment (Outz, 2006). McMillan and Chavis (1986) defined sense of community as "a feeling that members have of belonging, a feeling that members matter to one another and to the group, and a shared faith that members' needs will be met through their commitment to be together." (p. 9) Rovai (2002c) expanded on the definition of sense of community to suggest sense of community refers to the shared goals and values of group members, which promotes the feeling that individuals are members of a larger group. Rovai further defined the four dimensions that constitute classroom community: spirit, trust, interaction, and commonality of expectations and goals (i. e., learning). Spirit is the sense of being connected to the group. It is the sense of cohesion and the bond learners feel when they work together. Trust develops when students rely on one another and feel safe with each other. Trust enables students to open up and expose themselves during the learning process while feeling others will provide support. Interaction refers to the pattern of exchange and communicaton among other learners and the instructor. There is ample research which shows interaction is a key element in building a sense of community, particularly in online learning environments (McInnerney & Roberts, 2008; Overbaugh & Nickel, 2010; Swan 2002, 2003). Rovai (2002c) explain the final facet of classroom community is learning. Learning reflects the commonality of expectations and goals of the students by means of their commitment to a common educational purpose.

Justification for the Study

Past research has revealed that sense of community has a profound influence on a student's learning experiences (Dawson, 2006; Liu, Magjuka, Bonk, & Lee, 2007). There is specific research that reveals sense of community, which is gained through interaction and collaboration among the learners, plays a significant role in promoting a successful online learning experience among graduate students (Dawson, 2006, 2008; Liu, Magjuka, Bonk, & Lee, 2007; Rovai, 2002; Rovai & Jordan, 2004).

Haythornthwaite, Kazmer, Robins, and Shoemaker (2000) conducted a qualitative, longitudinal study that explored social support and community among members of a computer-supported distance learning program. The study explored how students created and maintained interpersonal relationships in an online environment. The study also assessed whether those relationships fostered a sense of community for the students. The sample of participants (N = 17) consisted of graduate students enrolled in a master's degree program at a university. The participants were enrolled in the Library Education Experimental Program of the Graduate School of Library and Information Science, at the University of Illinois (Haythornthwaite et al., 2000). The participants were interviewed at length over a period of one year. The interview questions focused on issues of support and community development among the participants in the program. The questions also focused on the participant's interaction patterns. For example, some questions asked whether participants worked on class assignments together, whether they socialized with their classmates both online and outside of the classroom, and whether they exchanged ideas and advice.

Haythornthwaite et al. (2000) used a grounded theory approach to collect and analyze data for the study. After each set of interviews, hypotheses were formulated and further questions were developed for use in subsequent interviews. The data were coded based on themes that emerged from the participants' responses. The findings revealed, over the course of one-year, the participants gradually developed and fostered a sense of community. Some participants developed personal ties with other members at the beginning of the program and sustained the ties throughout the program. The analysis of the interviews showed that sense of community was built through sharing ideas and experiences. One student reported it was the exchange of ideas during times of uncertainty with her classmates that she knew she was not alone as they too were experiencing the same difficulties (Hawthornthwaite et al.). The findings indicated interaction and communication among participants fostered the sense of community among the students (Haythornthwaite et al.).

In another study, Rovai and Jordan (2004) used a quantitative, causal-comparative design to examine the differences between perceived sense of community in a traditional classroom, a blended learning environment, and a fully online learning environment. Sense of community was measured using the Classroom Community Scale (CCS) developed by Rovai (2002). The CCS was used to measure classroom community, connectedness, and learning. The sample of participants (N = 68) consisted of graduate students enrolled in three graduate-level educational courses from a small accredited university in an urban southeastern setting. Participants were enrolled in courses during the same semester (Rovai & Jordan, 2004).

Rovai and Jordan (2004) hypothesized that a sense of community would be strongest in the blended course. Rovai and Jordan's reasoning behind their hypothesis was that a "combination of face-to-face and online learning environments provides a greater range of opportunities for students to interact with each other and with their professor. " (p. 4) When students feel connected to their peers in either learning environment: face-to-face and online environments, they tend to have a stronger sense of community, as they share ideas and goals in this learning community. The findings from Jordan and Rovai revealed the participants in the blended learning environment maintained a higher sense of connectedness than those in the face-to-face and online environments. Participants in the blended environment also scored higher on the learning sub-scale on the CCS than those in the online environment. One student commented in the end-of-the-course evaluation, which summarized the student's overall sense of community: "I would not have made it through this semester without the practical guidance of this course along with the freedom of the online component." The face-to-face interaction of the blended learning format coupled with the online component allowed the participants to build professional relationships, share ideas and experiences, and build upon their skills from the course such as implementing a management plan or using a new academic strategy, which as first learned online and had practical experience during the face-to-face class time. This type of interaction from the blended learning environment fostered a greater sense of community.

Other research has investigated sense of community in undergraduate degree programs. Pigliapoco and Bogliolo (2007) used as a case study approach to investigate sense of community of undergraduate students enrolled a degree program in Applied Computer Science. The program was offered by the university as a distance education course and as a non-campus course. Pigliapoco and Bogliolo examined the role of interaction and its effect on psychological sense of community (PSoC). PSoC represented the feelings of belonging and the shared values and commitment a member felt to the group. The PSoC was expressed by two indicators: *membership and SCITT* (spirit, commonality, interaction, trust granted, and trust received).

The Pigliapoco and Bogliolo (2007) study included students in online courses and students in face-to-face (F2F) courses. The sample consisted of 57 and 50 participants, respectively, enrolled in a bachelor's degree program. The data was collected at the end of the first semester of the program using an online questionnaire developed by Pigliapoco and Bogliolo. The questionnaire consisted of questions related to the students' personal profile such as academic experience, motivation, interests, and etc.; satisfaction of their degree program; and the students' PSoC (Pigliapoco & Bogliolo, 2007). The questionnaire was found to be reliable using Cronbach's alpha coefficient, 0.75 for the PSoC questions (Pigliapoco and Bogliolo, 2007).

Pigliapoco and Bogliolo (2007) compared to the two groups, online and F2F, in terms of sample average and standard deviation. The researchers also used multiple linear regression to determine if PSoC influenced the participant's performance, satisfaction, and persistence in the course groups. Using comparative analysis between the online group and the F2F group, the results revealed the online group experienced less uniform feelings of community than the F2F group.

Results further revealed the online students had a program dropout rate of over 50% where the students decided to drop out of their studies after their first academic year. The dropout rate of the F2F group was approximately 18%. Pigliapoco and Bogliolo's suggested the lack of PSoC may have been influenced to the lack of physical interaction among the online students. Pigliapoco and Bogliolo (2007) also suggested the online group may have experienced more difficulties based on work and family responsibilities independent of their personal satisfaction of the course and degree program. In contrast, the F2F students drop out typically when they feel unsatisfied with their choices in course or degree program (Pigliapoco & Bogliolo). Pigliapoco and Bogliolo suggested to reduce student isolation and alienation, online courses must help students feel a sense of belonging and connectedness to the group. This connection or sense of belonging may help foster the psychological sense of community among the students. Results also revealed the F2F group was six times likely to consider their colleagues as friends than the online group. Pigliapoco and Bogliolo suggested students are more likely to become friends when they meet regularly in a F2F class compared to the lack of physical contact in an online class. The regression analysis further revealed that PSoC was affected by the students' interest in the subject of the course as well as the interaction between their classmates in both learning environments. Pigliapoco and Bogliolo suggested that when students are motivated, interact with others, and receive timely feedback from their instructor on their assignments, they are more likely to feel a sense of community.

Pigliapoco & Bogliolo (2007) also compared the two groups on demographic characteristics. Based on the comparative analysis of both groups, results showed the online group was comprised mostly of full-time workers over the age of 30. The F2F group consisted of mostly full-time students under the age of 20 (Pigliapoco & Bogliolo, 2007). The variable that had the most impact on the number of exams passed and course grades was the teaching method. For example, there was a positive correlation with average marks (0.388) and a negative correlation with passed exams (-0.404). The online students passed fewer exams with better grades.

Research has revealed than non-traditional students tend to be more highly motivated and received better grades than the younger more traditional students (Pigliapoco & Bogliolo, 2007). The regression analysis revealed a negative correlation for hours work per day of -

0.337 and a positive correlation of hours studied per day of 0.181. With regard to the indicator of SCITT, there was a low correlation of hours worked per day of both groups, 0. 106 and a negative correlation of membership, -.0137 (Pigliapoco & Bogliolo).

Several quantitative studies (Adbous & Yen, 2010; Bollinger & Martindale, 2004;) have indicated course room interaction is related to positive student learning outcomes and student satisfaction. Few, if any, studies have addressed sense of community among community college students. The purpose of this study is to address this gap in the literature by investigating sense of community in community college students. The study will seek to determine if community college students in online, hybrid, and traditional courses differ in their sense of community.

Growth of Online Education

Online learning refers to "an approach to teaching and learning that utilizes Internet technologies to communicate and collaborate in an educational context" (Blackboard, 1998). Dwyer, Barbieri, and Doerr (1995) acknowledged the web is revolutionizing forums for communicating with others and increased opportunities for learning (Allen & Seaman, 2010). Online learning provides opportunities for communication and interaction between class members and faculty through discussion boards, chat rooms, and e-mail (Blackboard, 1998).

Online education has become very popular in recent years from its flexibility that allows access to course content to be presented anytime and anywhere. Results from recent surveys conducted by Allen and Seaman (2003, 2006, 2007, & 2010) and the findings from the NCES (1999 & 2008) demonstrates education is moving progressively more toward online programs. The results showed the number of institutions which offer online courses or degree programs is steadily increasng. The NCES (1999) reported the use of asynchronous Internet-based technologies grew from 22% of institutions in 1995 to 60% of institutions in 1997 – 1998. In 2003, 81% higher education institutions offered at least one fully online or blended course (Allen & Seaman, 2003). In the 2006-2007 academic year, 62-66% of institutions offered some type of distance edcuation course (Allen & Seaman, 2006; NCES, 2008).

Recent surveys from the Sloan Consortium demonstrated students pursuing higher education are moving progressively more toward online programs (Allen & Seaman, 2010). One study (Allen & Seaman, 2010b) revealed more than one in four higher education students take at least one online course. The survey also revealed over 4.6 million students took at least one online course during the fall 2008 term. The number of students who took online courses in 2008 was a substantial increase from the 3.5 million students in the fall of 2006 and the 2.3 million students in 2004 (Allen & Seaman, 2003, 2006). Research has indicated there has been a 21% growth rate for online enrollments in higher education, and that rate exceeded the 2% growth in the overall enrollment of students in higher education (Allen & Seaman, 2010).

The Instructional Technology Council [ITC] (Lokke & Womer, 2007) provided further evidence of the growing number of online courses being offered in higher education. The ITC developed an annual distance education survey to collect national data on the growing trends in distance education and e-learning. Data from the survey reported the growth in distance education is outpacing the growth rate of traditional enrollments. The data revealed a 15% increase in the 2004-2005 distance education enrollments, which was substantially higher than the overall campus enrollments. Even though the ITC's survey used the broad term of distance education to represent online learning, ITC reported 70% of distance education administrators reported the demand for distance education courses is exceeding their capacity to deliver such courses (Lokke & Womer, 2007). The following section discusses the benefits and drawbacks to online education as many turn to this delivery method for education.

Benefits of Online Learning

Online learning has some benefits that entice the students to this learning environment. O'Lawrence (2007) pointed out it is the "timelessness, dependability, and flexibility" of online learning is one main benefit of online learning. Many online students have to juggle both family and work responsibilities. Online students can arrange their learning schedule around their lives that include both work and family responsibilities without the barriers of time and place (Huang, 2002).

Some other benefits of online learning are the financial savings that can accrue compared to attending a traditional-land-based campus. For example, the distance to travel may be too great to attend school or the student may not have a vehicle to get to school. Learning online can reduce the transportation issues and the cost transportation (such as rising gas prices or the wear and tear on one's vehicle) if the student had to travel long distances to a college campus. There is the issue for some students with children. If the student cannot afford childcare or does not have a babysitter to care for their children while they are in school, this may prevent or limit the opportunity to continue their education. Online education allows students to continue their education without interfering with family responsibilities, jobs, and career paths (O'Lawrence, 2007).

Barriers to Online Learning

While there are many benefits to online learning, there are some barriers to learning online such as feelings of isolation or the feeling of being disconnected from their peers (Rovai & Wighting, 2005). Online learning lacks the physical-social interaction that exists in the traditional classroom, therefore students may experience feelings of being isolated and disconnected. The feelings of isolation and loneliness may lead to a negative learning experience (Outzs, 2006; Rovai & Wighting, 2005). Consequently, the feelings of isolation may lead to some students dropping out of online courses and perhaps dropping out of college (Rovai, 2002; Rovai, 2004; Rovai & Wighting, 2005). Research by Hawthornthwaite, Kazmer, Robins, and Shoemaker (2000) has shown feelings of isolation are related to a low sense of community experienced by some students online.

Outzs (2006) examined the issue of students' sense of isolation and disconnect in an online learning environment. Outzs used a nonexperimental, descriptive mixed-method research design to examine students' perception of sense of community in an online learning environment. The participants consisted of a convenience sample (N = 227) of online students from a western land-grant university. Of 820 eligible students, 227 students completed and submitted the Web-based survey; giving a response rate of 27.7%. Outzs used the Classroom Community Scale (CCS) developed by Dr. Rovai (2002) to examine sense of community. The online version of the CCS was hosted by the eCollege server of the university and disseminated to the students online.

Outzs (2006) coded the total scores for each scale of the CCS (classroom community, connected, and learning) as *low*, *mid*, and *high*. The students who had either low or high scores on the CCS were invited to participate in a semi-structured interview. Ten participants were selected in the semi-structured interview. Of the ten students, three students scored low on the CCS and seven students scored high on the CCS (Outzs, 2006). Outz used the interviews to gather qualitative data regarding students' experiences regarding sense of community in their online courses. When Outz examined the data from the semi-structured interviews, certain patterns emerged from the 10 students regarding their experiences of sense of community in online courses.

Analysis of data from the students rated as having a low sense of community revealed several common themes: poor teacher characteristics, low student-to-student connections, poor quality of learning, and a basic dissatisfaction of the course (Outzs, 2006). The students who had indicated a low sense of community typically said their learning experience was miserable. They indicated interactions between the students and the students to teachers were minimal during the courses. They further indicated the courses did not require collaborative learning. One student stated, "there was absolutely no interaction between students except in the chat rooms," and students frequently asked each other, "if anyone had heard from the instructor." (Outzs, 2006).

Students in the Outzs (2006) study who had given high scores for sense of community reported a positive learning experience. Data from students with a high sense of community revealed positive aspects of the course such as good teacher characteristics, strong student connection related to assignments, a change in personal perspective, quality learning, and satisfaction with the course (Outzs). The students reported having experienced positive interactions between students as well as between students and the instructor (Outzs).

Non-traditional College Students and Online Learning

The student population for most community colleges usually consists of non-traditional, low-income, and minority students (Provasnik & Planty, 2008). According to Cross (1980), Benshoff and Lewis (1992), and Hemby (1998), a non-traditional student is an adult who returns to school full- or part-time while maintaining responsibilities such as employment, family, and other responsibilities of adult life. A large percentage of community college students fit into the non-traditional category (IES, 2009). For example, 36% of the study body of one rural community college in Down East Maine is approximately 25 years of age or older (Washington County Community College [WCCC], 2010).

Qureshi, Morton, and Antonsz (2002) conducted a quantitative study that revealed some differences in the demographic characteristics of students in web-based courses and students in F2F courses. The data showed web-based courses seemed to attract more non-traditional students with family and work responsibilities. A larger percentage of the web-based students were married with children. The findings revealed 30.4% of the web-based students were married compared to 12.6% for the traditional students. Results also showed students in the web-based courses were more likely to have children and have higher incomes. Results showed that 90.5% of on-campus students the students had dependents compared to 77.2% of web-based students (Qureshi et al., 2002).

Findings from Qureshi et al.'s study also demonstrated that online students had more challenges with respect to work responsibilities. For example, 20.35% of the online students worked full-time compared to the 8.4% of the on-campus students. This study was substantiated by later research which indicated online students are typically older and work full-time when compared to traditional students who live on-campus (Taniguchi & Kaufman, 2007).

Non-traditional age students may face more challenges with regard to navigating the technology associated with technology than their younger traditional age counterparts. For example, a large percentage of the community college population consists of Baby Boomers (individuals born 1943 through 1960) (Emeagwali, 2007). These non-traditional students may face electronic and technological challenges due to less exposure to technology (FBI National Executive Institute, 2007). The generation of Baby Boomers grew up before the proliferation of computers and electronics, and they may not be skilled in the use of electronic mediums afforded by computers. Boomers may prefer to use more familiar technology such as the traditional telephone versus using newer technology such as the cellular phone (Rodriguez, Green, & Ree, 2003).

In contrast, younger students who are from Generation X (individuals born between 1960 and 1980), tend to be far more advanced in their technological skills

(Rodriquez et al., 2003). This generation grew up during the time of technological explosions and advancement. Therefore, students from Generation X may be very comfortable using technical mediums such as surfing the Internet and communicating through e-mail, beepers, and cellular phones (Rodriquez et al.).

Beyth-Marom, Chajut, Roccas, and Sagiv (2003) have conducted research which has shown age to be a factor that is correlated with levels of computer anxiety. Beth-Marom et al. found students in an Internet-assisted learning environment (IDL; the blending of a traditional-land-based course and online technology) had a higher academic achievement compared to students in a traditional distance learning environment (TDL). Students in the IDL group were a blend of younger students (10.8%) (students< 20 years of age) and older students (59.8%) (31-40 years of age). However, the TDL group was composed 4.0% younger students (students< 20 years of age) and 74.6% of the students were (1-40 years of age. The average grade of students in the IDL group (79.52) was significantly higher ($t(822) = 2.87$, $p < 0.01$) than the average grade in the TDL group (76.03) (Beth-Marom et al.). The students were in the course *Introduction to Statistics*. Beth-Marom et al. examined if age and grades had a connection. The IDL students had a higher GPA in all age groups. There were significant differences for age ranges of 20-30, 340-40, and 50-60 ($p < 0.001$, $p < 0.05$, $p < 0.01$, respectively). Beth-Marom et al. denote higher grades in statistics may be related to less math anxiety and computer anxiety. Hemby (1998) found non-traditional students do not necessarily show more computer anxiety. He proposed computer anxiety may not stem from anxiety related to technology; rather the anxiety may be related to a lack of self-directedness in learning. Hemby suggested that non-traditional students who are more self-directed in their learning are also less anxious in online learning environments that foster this self-directed learning style.

Theoretical Foundation

The theoretical foundation for this study was social constructivism, which emphasizes how social interactions with others enhance the learning process. Research has shown optimal learning occurs in a constructivist setting (Jonassen, Peck, & Wilson, 1999; Kasworm, 2003; Vygostky, 1978). Humans are social creatures, and for this reason humans tend to grow and develop through social interactions in a variety of communities (Woo & Reeves, 2007). According to Vygotsky (1978) all cognitive functions are viewed as products of the interactions of others. The types of interactions in a classroom include discussion with other students, interactions with the teacher, etc. Learning is primarily a social process. Students' conversations with their classmates allow them to share their backgrounds and participate in the give and take of collaborative and cooperative activities (Sthapornnanon, Sakulbumrungsil, Theeraroungchaisri & Watcharadamrongkun, 2009). Woo and Reeves (2007) admit not all conversations and discussions result in meaningful learning. Meaningful interaction consists of sharing and responding to ideas. It is negotiating both internally and socially among the class members. It also allows one to defend one's ideas and offers alternative perspectives when individuals engage in relevant collaborative activities (Vygotsky, 1978; Woo & Reeves, 2007).

The theory of social constructivism has primarily been used for the traditional classroom. However, as online classrooms begin to develop and grow, the principles of constructivism can also be used to explain how sense of community is developed in online and hybrid courses. Redfern and Naughton (2002) stated learning is not achieved as an "isolated individual act, but a collective result of social interaction" (p. 2). For this social interaction to occur and learning to occur, a sense of community must be built (Redfern & Naughton, 2002; Rovai & Wighting, 2005; Shea, 2006).

Social constructivism is a philosophy of learning based on how knowledge is constructed by the individual through interaction with the environment (Huang, 2002; Rovai, 2004). Constructivism was influenced by Dewey (1916), Piaget (1973), and Vygotsky (1978). Dewey (1916) proposed that knowledge is through the individual's experiences with the environment. Dewey believed the role of teacher was to guide learning through interaction. Teachers main purpose is to communicate knowledge and skills; they also guide students in creating their own knowledge (Dewey, 1938). Meaning and knowledge construction is achieved by making connections with other things and other individuals through the process of interaction. Both Piaget and Dewey believed the teacher helped shape the individual's real experiences with the environment (Huang, 2002; Ornstein & Hunkins, 1998).

Vygostky focused on the effects of social interaction, language, and culture on learning (Vygotsky, 1978; Woo & Reeves, 2007). Vygotsky believed psychological development and instruction is achieved and embedded on a social plane through dialogue (Vygotsky, 1978). Vygotsky proposed that meaning is constructed through the process of sharing of perspectives and experiences through collaborative relationship (Rovai & Wighting, 2005; Vygotsky, 1978; Woo & Reeves, 2007).

Vygotsky's (1978) conception of social constructivism provides the foundation for the proposed study. Vygotsky (1978) believed "human learning presupposes a specific social nature" (p. 88), and he emphasized students do not learn in isolation but rather through collaboration within social environments (Huang, 2002; Moll, 1990). The collaboration and interaction between both students and instructors enables students to perceive they are part of a shared learning community. Students who feel isolated and alienated in their courses due to lack of interaction with their teachers and other students may lack a sense of classroom community (Rovai & Wighting, 2005).

Learning is a result of active social interaction among learners (Rovai & Wighting, 2005). Learning is achieved when there is a strong sense of community among its members (Rovai & Wighting, 2005). For this reason, educators and instructional designers need to develop collaborative activities and online instructional strategies that foster this social interaction and promote a strong sense of community among the students. Student-to-student as well as instructor-to-student interaction will help reduce feelings of isolation and promote high achievement among all students (Rovai & Wighting, 2005).

Sense of Community in a Constructivist Setting

The building of knowledge results from active social interaction among learners (Rovai & Wighting, 2005). For the social constructivist, the social interaction and the social context provide the bases for which individuals gain knowledge and create meaning from social activities. Rovai and Wighting (2005) contend learning occurs most effectively when there is a strong sense of community among its members. Collaborative activities facilitate and promote social interaction and have potential for reducing feelings of isolation and increasing sense of community (Rovai & Wighting, 2005).

Developing a Community through Interaction

According to Schweir and Balbar (2002) and Weasenforth, Biesenbach-Lucas, and Meloni (2002) effective learning communities are founded on social constructivist pedagogy and promote online learning communities. When students are engaged in learning by negotiating, co-creating, and expanding meaning in an online environment, learning is achieved. This type of learning supports the social constructivist perspective of how meaning is constructed and how learning occurs (Lee, Carter-Wells, Glaeser, Ivers, and Street (2006).

Kasworm (2003) conducted a qualitative study that explored adult learners' beliefs about how they constructed knowledge in the classroom and the relationship of that knowledge to their broader life involvements. The sample (N = 90) consisted of adult undergraduate students from a community college, a liberal arts college, and a university. Semi-structured interviews were used to collect data. A purposeful sampling strategy was used to identify those individuals who were (a) at least 30 years of age, (b) were in good academic standing, (c) were currently enrolled in a baccalaureate program or in a college transfer program at the community college, and (d) had completed at least 15 hours of academic coursework at each institution. Based on the interviews, Kasworm found three key factors played a role in how the learners constructed meaning in the classroom: the classroom, the nature of the knowledge or how the learner views the knowledge in relationship to their own experiences, and the instructor's role in the course. The participants in Kasworm's (2003) study identified the classroom as the main forum for the creation of knowledge. For adult learners, the classroom defined their college experiences. For example, the college experience was based on the learner's personal beliefs about how college was supposed to be rather than how it actually was. The non-traditional students did not typically identify a peer group or view their campus experience as having a significant influence on their college experience. The adult learners defined their classroom learning experience according to their own lives outside of the classroom (Kasworm).

Kasworm's (2003) study further revealed interactions with the instructors and other students influenced the learners' negotiation of meaning of course content. Some of the participants acknowledged as they engaged in discussion with their peers and the instructor, interactions assisted the participants to integrate information into their already existing knowledge. Some participants revealed how their interactions with the instructor challenged their own beliefs and perspectives. The participants elaborated on how those challenges enabled them to construct new knowledge and meaning (Kasworm).

According to Lee, Carter-Wells, Glaeser, Ivers, and Street (2006), positive interactions with others provides opportunities for students to construct meaning or gain an understanding when they do not necessarily understand the course concepts. Lee et al. conducted a qualitative study to investigate the phenomenon of online community development. The researchers conducted a case study of a cohort of 18 students in an instructional design and technology graduate online program. Lee et al. collected secondary data from online discussion boards, student's reflective journals, focus groups, and a web-based survey. The data from the mulitple sources were analyzed using a research team and triangulation to determine to what extent the characterisitcs of effective online learning communities converged with or diverged with students' perceptions of community (Lee et al.).

Results from Lee et al. (2006) revealed 93% of the students reported they strongly agreed or agreed they participated in a constructivist learning environment. The participants reported they had explored, experimented, and engaged in active learning activities that provided them with information they were able to apply to practice. For example, Lee et al. reported one student stated, "my interactions with other students, watching other students ahead or behind me on the path, allowed me to revisist my learning in the same or slightly different way." (p. 19)

Through the process of interacting with others, students have an opportunity to grasp concepts and ideas, especially when they did not understand the material. Students are able to construct new meaning based on interaction with peers (Lee et al., 2006; Woo & Reeves, 2007). Also, 74% of students reported using social networking to reduce their feelings of isolation and feel more connected with their peers (Lee et al., 2006). It is important to note while students reported positive interactions fostered their sense of community, only 26% indicated the most meaningful learning came from interaction with peers. Synthesizing the interviews and triangulating the data, Lee et al. 's study found when students are engaged in multiple discussion forums such as discussion boards, social networks, and chat room, in an online learning enviroment, it fostered a knowledge building community.

Sense of Community and Student Success

Past research has indicated that sense of community plays a distinct role in students' academic success. Sense of community contributes to students' motivation, increases learning, reduces feelings' of isolation, and increases retention (Boston, Diaz, Gibson, Ice, Richardson, & Swan, 2009; Shen, Nuankhieo, Amelung, & Laffey, 2008; Wighting, Liu, & Rovai, 2008).

Motivation

Wighting, Liu, and Rovai (2008) examined motivation and sense of community among two groups of students (N = 353) using a quantitative, correlational design. The first group of students was enrolled in e-learning courses and the other group was enrolled in face-to-face (F2F) university courses. A total of 24 courses were involved in the study: 12 online and 12 F2F. Wighting et al. used discriminant analysis to classify students according to what type of course in which they were enrolled. Wighting et al. sought to examine if certain variables (classroom community, classroom learning community, school social community, intrinsic motivation, extrinsic motivation, and amotivation) could be used to classify students according to their enrollment in either online or F2F courses. The Classroom and School Community Inventory (CSCI) and the 28-item Academic Motivation Scale College (AMS-C 28) were used to collect data on the variables of interest.

The CCSI was used to measure classroom community and school community (Wighting et al., 2008). The CCSI consisted of 10 self-report items for the classroom community scale and ten self-report items for the school community scale. Respondents used a 5-point Likert scale to respond to the items on the survey. The possible responses for each item were *strongly agree* = 4, *agree* = 3, *neutral* = 2l, *disagree* = 1, and *strongly disagree* = 0. The CCSI had a total possible combined score of 0 to 40 for classroom community and school community. Higher scores on the scale reflected a stronger sense of community. Total scores were calculated by adding points assigned to each of the items assigned to each scale (Wighting et al.)

The AMS-C 28 was used to measure intrinsic, extrinsic, and amotivation in college students (Wighting et al., 2008). Students responded to items of the AMS-C28 using a 7-point Likert scale. Responses on the scale ranged from 1 (*does not correspond at all*) to seven (*corresponds exactly*) (Wighting et al., 2008). Twelve of the items within the AMS-C 28 measured intrinsic motivation, twelve measured extrinsic motivation, and four measured amotivation. The scales for intrinsic and extrinsic ranged from a low of 12 to a high of 84, and amotivation, from a low of 4 to a high of 28.

Results (Wighting et al., 2008) from the discriminant analysis found that classroom social community $F(1, 318) = 17.97$, $p < .001$, school learning community, $F(1, 318) = 8.76$, $p < .003$, and intrinsic motivation, $F(1, 318)$, 18.35, $p < .001$, were significant predictors of course enrollment category for students in online and traditional land-based courses. The results also revealed intrinsic motivation was the best predictor in determining which type of course in which a student was enrolled. Other findings revealed intrinsic motivation was the strongest predictor of group membership for the online group followed by classroom social community and school learning community (Wighting et al.). On the whole, results from the study revealed online learners had more intrinsic motivation than F2F learners.

Qureshi, Morton, and Antosz (2002) evaluated the differences in motivational orientation between students ($N = 240$) enrolled in a web-based course and in a traditional F2F course. One hundred-twenty students were randomly selected from four web-based courses to participate in the study. Another 120 students were randomly selected from the students enrolled in on-campus courses (Qureshi et al.). The total sample contained 240 students.

In contrast to previous findings, Qureshi et al. (2002) conducted a study which showed web-based students to be less motivated than their F2F counterparts. Qureshi et al. used a questionnaire to identify characteristics of students that were enrolled in a distance education program. The questionnaire included 55 items distributed across four sections: section one collected data on demographic characteristics (age, gender, marital status, etc.); section two captured data on computer skills and experience (application of software, e-mail exchange, knowledge of the Internet, etc.); section three assessed student motivation to enroll in an online course or a traditional F2F course; and section four collected information on any challenges or barriers the student experienced during the course (such as learning style preference or educational barriers). Participants rated themselves using a 5-point, Likert-type scale where responses ranged from *1 = strongly agree* to *5 = strongly disagree*. The lower scores were viewed more positive.

A discriminant function analysis was used to examine differences between the two groups (Web-based students and F2F students) with regard to course experiences, motivation, and barriers to academic success. Qureshi et al. (2002) found web-based students were less motivated than counterparts in F2F course(s) as indicated by the means and standard deviations. For example, the motivation to acquire knowledge was M = 3.44, SD = 1.5 for the web-based courses and *M* = 3.44, *SD* = 1.05 compared to the F2F course, *M* = 3.22, *SD* = 1.02. Qureshi et al. offered a few possible explanations for the contradictory findings. First, the F2F students were willing to invest more time and effort in their studies. Second, the higher motivation for the F2F students might may been due to the influence of peers, presence of an audience, and the face-to-face experiences, which are all aspects of traditional courses. Qureshi et al. acknowledged people perform better when someone else is watching them. Based in this study, intrinsic motivation was an important indicator for online students.

Feelings of Connectedness

A sense of connectedness and shared values among students allows students to actively pursue knowledge in the online learning environment and achieve academic success. Researchers (Rovai & Wighting, 2005) suggest that students in online courses may be more likely to experience isolation and alienation when there is a lack of meaningful interaction due to a physical separation from the school and its services and from other students.

Rovai and Wighting (2005) examined sense of community and feelings of alienation among online students. The researchers used a convenience sample (*N* = 117) of graduate students enrolled in online, educational-research method courses. Rovai and Wighting used the Dean Alienation Scale (Dean, 1961) to operationalize the construct of alienation. The Dean Alienation Scale is a self-reporting instrument consisting of 24 items which examined a person's feelings of alienation in a non-situational context. Dean (1961) used generic statements to draw out an individual's perception of social isolation as opposed to a more situational nature such as, "*my educational future looks very dismissal.*" Some examples of statements that addressed non-situational contexts include: *the future looks very dismal*, *the world in which we live is basically a friendly place*, and *people's ideas change so much that I wonder if we'll ever have anything to depend on* (Rovai & Wighting). Each statement referred to a generic situation. Participants used a 5-point, Likert-type scale, to rate themselves on each item of the instrument. The possible responses ranged from *strongly agree = 5, agree = 4, uncertain = 3, disagree = 2,* and *strongly disagree = 1.*

The Dean Alienation Scale (Dean, 1961) has three sub-scales that measure social isolation, powerlessness, and normlessness. The social isolation and powerlessness sub-scales each consisted of nine items, while the sub-scale normlessness consisted of six items. The sub-scales were calculated by adding the Likert scale ratings for each of the items assigned to each scale. The potential scores ranged from a low of nine to a high of 45 for social isolation and powerlessness and from six to 30 for normlessness (Rovai & Wighting, 2005).

The Classroom Community Scale (Rovai, 2002) was used to measure classroom community. The CCS is a 20-item Likert-type scale that provided a total score for three scales: *classroom community, connectedness,* and *learning* (Rovai, 2002). The total possible score for the CCS ranges from 0-80, with higher scores reflecting a stronger sense of community. Chapter 3 will present the details of the CCS. The Dean Alienation Scale and the CCS were provided to the online students in the final weeks of the course as an online survey using the Blackboard e-learning system (Rovai & Wighting, 2005).

Rovai and Wighting used a quantitative, correlational design to determine how the three alienation sub-scales (social isolation, powerlessness, and normlessness) were related to the two classroom community scales (connectedness and learning). Canonical correlation analysis (CCA) was used to analyze the data. Significant relationships were found between the three alienation variables and the two classroom community variables. The findings indicated a student's sense of alienation and isolation was inversely related to the student's sense of community. Participants with both stronger feelings of social isolation and powerlessness were also likely to have a weaker sense of connectedness and learning (Rovai & Wighting, 2005). Findings from the study suggests when a student feels a sense of alienation and isolation in an online class, the student is not likely to develop a strong sense of community.

Rovai and Wighting's (2005) study highlights the importance of reducing a student's sense of alienation and isolation in an online course. Rovai (2001) suggests using interaction to alleviate the feelings of loneliness and isolation experienced by students in online courses. Interaction is an important element in the learning process.

Increased Learning

Rovai (2002c) reported there is a relationship between sense of community and learning in online education. As discussed earlier, learning is the second component of classroom community, when members of a learning community feel connected to each other and to the group as a whole, there is the feeling that knowledge and meaning can be actively constructed in that learning community (Rovai, 2000c). Ultimately, the goal of the learning community is to learn.

Rovai (2002c) examined sense of community and cognitive learning to determine if there was a relationship between the two variables. Rovai used a convenience sample (N = 314) of graduate students enrolled in 26 online courses during one semester (15 weeks). Rovai used the CCS (Rovai, 2002) and a self-report measure (Richmond, Gorham, & McCroskey, 1987) to measure the students perceived cognitive learning.

The Classroom Community Scale (Rovai, 2002) was used to measure classroom community. The CCS is a 20-item Likert-type scale that provided a total score for three scales: *classroom community*, *connectedness*, and *learning* (Rovai, 2002). The total possible score for the CCS ranges from 0-80, with higher scores reflecting a stronger sense of community. Chapter 3 will present the details of the CCS.

Rovai (2002c) used a self-report employed by Richmond et al., (1987) to measure perceived cognitive learning. Participants were asked to respond to one question: "On a scale of 0 to 9, how much did you learn in this class, with 0 meaning you learned nothing and 9 meaning you learned more than in any other class?" Rovai (2002c) pointed out since this was a single-item scale, no internal consistency reliability estimates were possible.

Rovai's (2002c) findings from a multiple regression analysis revealed the two sub-scales of the CCS, connectedness and learning, were significantly related to perceived cognitive learning, $F(2, 311) = 115.68, p < .001$. The two sub-scales explained 43% of the variance of perceived cognitive learning in the sample. Independent t tests revealed connectedness, $t(312) = 2.07, p = .04, \acute{\eta}^2 = .014$. and cognitive learning, $t(312) = 2.00, p = .048, \acute{\eta}^2 = .004$, were higher in the female participants (Rovai, 2002c). Rovai did note the strength of the relationship between gender and connectedness and perceived learning were weak as evaluated by $\acute{\eta}^2$.

Rovai's (2002c) findings do suggest there is a relationship between sense of community and learning. However, Rovai acknowledges this is not a causal relationship between sense of community and perceived learning. Rovai further acknowledged a higher sense of community it would not necessarily result in higher levels of cognitive learning. The findings of the study do suggest online graduate students do feel connected to their online classroom community. In addition, students with a stronger sense of community tend to possess a greater sense of perceived cognitive learning (Rovai, 2002c).

Retention

Researchers (Carr, 2000; Terry, 2001) reported there is minimal empirical evidence examining retention rates other than from individual academic institutions examining course completion and program retention rates. Carr (2000) reported retention rates in online distance learning courses ranged from 50% to 80%, while the rates for face-to-face courses typically range from 80%-90%. Terry (2001) studied business courses at West Texas A&M University and found the accounting, economics, computer information systems, marketing, and management had online attrition rates comparable to their face-to-face counterparts. In contrast, the business statistics and finance courses had online attrition rates between 33% and 48% while face-to-face classes had attrition rates between 13% and 23%. Moskal and Dziuban (2001) at the University of Central Florida found women were 8% more likely than men to succeed in online courses by completing the course with a grade of C or better. Online courses had higher withdrawal rates than face-to-face or combination courses about 8% of men and 6% of women withdrew (Moskal & Dziuban, 2001). The NCES (2011) reported in 2-year institutions, the retention rates for those who entered school in 2008 were 61% for full-time students and 40% for part-time students.

Researchers (Bocchi, Eastman, & Swift, 2004) have shown a team-based learning experience and extensive meaningful course interactions helps retain online learners. Bocchi et al. reported the Georgia WebMBA program has maintained an average retention rate of 89% for its cohorts beginning in 2001. The WebMBA program is offered by five universities in the University System of Georgia. The program consists of ten courses and admits only 35 students per cohort. The WebMBA program collects pre-orientation surveys to examine student characteristics in an effort to understand why the cohorts have a high retention rate. Results from the survey reported the students ranged in age from 30 to 35 years old with undergraduate degrees in business-related fields (Bocchi et al., 2004).

In 2001, two cohorts ($N = 35$ and $N = 29$) were asked to participant in an e-mailed survey (Bocchi et al, 2004). Each student was asked to rate on a five-point Likert-type scale, their degree of agreement or disagreement on the 23 possible reasons why they joined the WebMBA program. The findings from the survey revealed that many students decided to participate in online programs for geographical reasons. Participants also indicated the program matched their personal and professional goals, and their employer had positive views about the program (Bocchi et al., 2004). The findings also pointed out even though joining an accredited program was important not only to the student, but for the employer. Other reasons for joining the program were that the course worked for their work schedule and the program had 24-7 accessibility (Bocchi et al.).

Sense of Community and Interaction

Research has consistently revealed interactions between teacher and student, as well as student interactions their classmates, are crucial to the students' online learning (Rovai, 2001; Swan, 2002, 2003; Webb-Boyd, 2008; Woo & Reeves, 2007). Interaction among people with similar interests can create a learning community that, "… may be more stimulating, interesting, and intense for those involved" (Rovai, 2001, p. 32). Webb-Boyd (2008) examined the nature of student and teacher interactions among students in online and hyrid courses. The objective was to determine how course interactions affected student learning. The sample consisted of students from first-year composition courses at a large western university.

Webb-Boyd (2008) devised an online survey based on Chickering and Gamson's (1987) Seven Principles of Learner Centered Education. Chickering and Gamson focused on seven key principles promoted at the university and included: student-faculty contact; cooperation amond students; active learning; prompt instructor feedback; time on task; communication of high expectations; and respect for diverse talents and ways of learning as these principles are applied to online teaching and learning. Webb-Boyd (2008) reported approximately 52% of the students in both the online and hybrid writing courses reported that interaction with their instructors were higher than their interactions with instructors in F2F courses. Over 22% of students reported the interactions with their online instructors were about the same as with their F2F instructors. According to the findings of Webb-Boyd's survey, students indicated that feedback from the instructor on their assignments was the key to their learning. Students also indicated the turn-around time of when the instructors responded with feedback on assignments was also an important component of their learning. For example, 72% of the participants that asked for help from the teacher reported they received feedback within 24 hours (Webb-Boyd). Students further revealed feedback received from their instructor provided them with information on their class standing.

The findings of Webb-Boyd's (2008) survey also reported some of the sources of students' dissatisfaction with their courses. The dissatisfaction stemmed from the lack of clear expectations from the teacher in the online discussion assignments. Dissatisfaction came from how the students' participation influenced the overall course grade. For example, 41.4% of the students indicated they were not clear on the relationship of online participation and their grade (Webb-Boyd). When there is a lack of interaction such as information from the teacher and the students, online connections may be difficult to achieve making students feel isolated in the class (Graf, 2003). The lack of satisfaction some students reported in Webb-Boyd's study may stem from a lack of what Rovai (2002) explained as mutual interdependence and a sense of trust and interaction among community members. When the students do not receive an adequate amount of interaction from the teacher or other students, they may not experience a sense of community in the online class.

Dawson (2006) also conducted a quantitative study to examine the relationships between student communication and interactions with peers and their sense of community within an online learning environment. The various types of interactions consisted of student use of e-mail, telephone phone calls, online discussion forums to include chat rooms, text messaging, and face-to-face. Dawson's sample (N = 464) consisted of undergraduate and postgraduate students from a large Australian university. Dawson conducted survey research using the Classroom Community Scale (CCS) (Rovai, 2002) to quantify the degree of community experienced among the participants. Dawson found a significant relationship between students' sense of community and the cumulative frequency of communication between the students. Results from an ordinary least squares regression procedure produced an adjusted R^2 value of .242 with all modes of communication; thus indicating a significant, yet moderate, proportion of the variance in sense of community was accounted for by the variables (Dawson, 2006). The adjust R^2 value for *connectedness and learning community sub-scales* of the CCS was 0.271 and 0.140 respectively (Dawson, 2006). Modes of communication that were strong predictors of the students' overall sense of community and statistically significant were e-mail, face-to-face communication, and discussion forum postings. Conversely, the use of phone communications, online chat forums, and text messaging were not statistically significant predictors of the students' sense of community as measured by the CCS.

Dawson's (2006) study had potential limitations. First, the study was conducted at one institution and therefore the results may not be generalizable to a broader population. Second, there was a relatively low response rate to the CCS (Dawson, 2006). The survey was disseminated through both the online units of course study home page and via e-mail notification. For instance, 23% of the participants (N = 464) responded to the CCS. A low response rate reduces confidence in the data and the findings from the data may not be generalized to a larger population (Baruch & Holtom, 2008; Hoonakker & Carayon, 2009). According to Baruch and Holtom (2008), surveys with higher response rates lead to larger data samples that generally have more statistical power. When surveys have a higher response rates, the sample is more likely to represent the overall target population. Since Dawson's study had a relatively low response rate to the CCS, the results may not be generalizable to the larger population as indicated in Dawson's (2006) results.

In another study Liu, Magjuka, Bonk, and Lee (2007) used a mixed-methods, case study approach to explore participants' perceptions of building a learning community in graduate online courses. A basic assumption was made based on previous research (Dawson, 2006; Rovai & Wighting, 2005), which indicated online communities help students build social connections in an online course and thereby reduces feelings of isolation and alienation that students may feel while in an online course. Liu et al. chose an accredited online MBA program in a top-ranked business school in a Midwestern university to conduct the study. The qualitative aspect of the study consisted of interviews with faculty members and 20 second-year MBA students. Each semi-structured interview was a one-to-one format that lasted approximately 45- to 75-minutes. The interviews focused on students' online learning experience and sense of community.

The quantitative portion of the Liu et al. (2007) consisted of a secondary data analysis of program evaluation surveys conducted across the 27 online MBA courses. The program evaluations were conducted to assess the students' online learning experience, their sense of community, and their satisfaction with their courses (Liu et al., 2007). The program evaluation survey comprised 65 questions that addressed the student's overall perceptions and attitudes toward online learning. Participants responded to each item using a 5-point Likert type scale.

Liu et al. (2007) employed Strauss and Corbin's constant comparative method to triangulate the data from the interview transcripts to determine emerging themes that related to learning communities in online courses. To ensure reliability while coding the emerging themes from the interviews of the students, Liu et al. had two separate interview transcripts examined. The researchers examined two separate transcripts and coded the emerging themes independently. The researchers discussed any coding decisions to establish a common set of codes based on the transcripts examined. An inter-coder agreement of 89% was achieved. The data was coded again using qualitative software to determine the frequency of the various coding categories.

Findings from Liu et al.'s (2007) qualitative data analysis suggested the absence of interpersonal relationships and the teacher's lack of social presence in the online courses prevented some students from feeling as though they were in a learning community. For example, one student commented, "Because we don't understand each other's personalities ... for me the most difficult part of, and the worst part, the hardest part, is to try and understand who these other people are." This comment suggested the low sense of social presence in the online courses prevented some students from interacting and collaborating with other students in the online learning community.

Liu et al.'s (2007) results also reflected how the instructor's presence and facilitation skills in the classroom positively affected student performance. The results revealed a positive correlation existed between teacher's presence in the classroom and the students' perceived sense of community (r =. 0.46, p < .01). The results indicated when the instructor provided consistent feedback to the students such as regular course announcements and feedback on course assignments, the students tended to have a higher perceived sense of classroom community. The findings were consistent with previous research which revealed that teacher presence is associated with fostering s sense of community (Rovai, 2002; Shea, 2006).

Liu et al.'s (2007) quantitative findings from the program evaluation survey showed approximately 90% of the respondents (N = 102) either agreed or strongly agreed with the statement they were part of a learning community in their online courses. Data further showed 60% of the students gave responses which indicated they did not have a sense of isolation in the online course. Approximately 25% of participants did feel isolated. A positive correlation was found between feelings of belonging to the learning community and learning engagement (r = .62, p < .01). This finding further supports the notion that interaction among class members helps to reduce the feelings of alienation and isolation for students in online classes (Rovai, 2002c; Rovai & Wighting, 2005). An online learning environment has the potential to encourage communication so each student may get to know their fellow classmates and allow the students to express themselves more freely. This is not the case for every student.

Sense of Community in Various Learning Formats

Previous research has indicated there may be differences in how students in various learning environments perceive sense of community. Rovai and

Jordan (2004) used a causal-comparative design to examine the differences between perceived sense of community in the traditional classroom, blended learning environment, and a fully online learning environment. Sense of community in each of the three learning environments were measured using the Classroom Community Scale (CCS). Students in the traditional and blended learning environments completed the CCS during the face-to-face meetings with the instructor, while students in the online course completed the CCS via an online survey (Rovai & Jordan).

Rovai and Jordan (2004) hypothesized that sense of community would be strongest in the blended course. Rovai and Jordan's reasoning behind their hypothesis was that a, "… combination of face-to-face and online learning environments provides a greater range of opportunities for students to interact with each other and with their professor." (p. 4) The independent variable was the type of setting (traditional course, blended course, and fully online). The dependent variables were the CCS sub-scales of *connectedness* and *learning*. The connectedness sub-scale represented the students' feelings with regard to their sense of cohesion, trust, interdependence with their classmates. The learning sub-scale represented feelings of the community group with regard to the degree they shared educational goals and experienced benefits by interacting with their classmates (Rovai & Jordan, 2004).

Rovai and Jordan's (2004) sample of participants (N = 68) consisted of graduate students enrolled in three graduate-level education courses during the same semester from a small accredited university in an urban southeastern setting (Rovai & Jordan). A multivariate analysis of covariance (MANCOVA) was used to analyze the data. The findings from Rovai and Jordan revealed participants in the blended learning environment maintained higher feelings of connectedness than those in the face-to-face and online environments. Participants in the blended environment scored higher on the learning sub-scale than those in the online environment. The blended group experienced a greater sense of community when compared to the participants in the face-to-face and online courses. Rovai and Jordan found students in the blended course had the highest estimated marginal mean on the connectedness variable (M = 34.91), followed by students in the traditional course (M = 30.78). Students in the online course yielded the lowest marginal mean (M = 28.83) on the Connectedness Scale. The difference between the scores of participants of the traditional course and scores of participants in the online course was not significant.

Other findings from the study (Rovai & Jordan, 2004) found the dependent variables (*connectedness* and *learning*) were significantly affected by course type. The online course showed more diverse scores of connectedness and learning than either the traditional or blended courses. The distribution of connectedness and learning of the CCS among online students revealed a decidedly negative skew. Rovai and Jordan suggested the negative skew may have existed due to some confounding variables. These confounding variables may have been related to how a student learns as well as influence the perception of their sense of community in online courses. Rovai and Jordan suggested there may have been other factors that may have influenced their research results. Rovai and Jordan suggested a student's learning style, self-motivation, interest in the material presented in the course, support from the family, and learner's level of responsibility for their own learning (Irizarry, 2002) may factor in to the degree which a student experiences a sense of community.

According to Rovai and Jordan (2004), the variables that contributed to a greater overall sense of community for the students in the blended course could be summed up by the comments from one participant in the end-of-the-course evaluation: "I would not have made it through this semester without the practical guidance of this course along with the freedom of the online component." The face-to-face interaction coupled with the online interaction fostered a greater sense of community in the blended course than the other two learning environments (F2F or online). The interaction in both online and F2F courses provided opportunities for students to share ideas and experiences, and enabled them to build upon their educational and professional skills. Interaction among students and educators is a key factor in fostering r a greater sense of community (Arbaugh & Benbunan-Fich, 2007; McInnerney & Roberts, 2008; Overbaugh & Nickel, 2010; Swan 2002, 2003).

Rovai and Jordan (2004) indicated some limitations to the study. First, Rovai and Jordon's research was confined to only three courses at the same university. Therefore, the findings may not be generalizable to a broader population. Secondly, the course instruction, course content, course design, and pedagogy may not have been representative of the course instruction, content, course design, and pedagogy in other settings. For example, each instructor has their own style of conveying information. The design of the course and activities may not be consistent with each instructor as each instructor may design the course differently than another. Furthermore, Rovai and Jordan did not confirm that cause and effect relationships might have occurred. Lastly, the researchers did not have an experimental control over the courses in which they conducted research. Rovai and

Jordan did not control for events that would occur in the classroom which could have affected the outcomes of the study. Rovai and Jordan were not the instructors of the courses. Since they were not the instructors, student exposure to the independent variables could not be controlled.

In another study, Ritter, Polnick, Fink, and Oescher (2010) also found a greater sense of community in the traditional and blended courses than online courses. Ritter et al. examined three delivery methods (face-to-face, hybrid, and online) to determine if there any differences in how each environment stimulated sense of community among students. Ritter et al. sought to determine if there were any statistically significant differences in the way each of these different learning environments promoted connectedness and learning.

Ritter et al. (2010) used a quantitative survey design to measure participants' sense of community as indicated by their sense of *connectedness* and *learning*. The survey was disseminated using the university's e-mail system to graduate students from 12 educational leadership courses. One hundred twenty-six students completed the survey, which reflected a response rate of 88%. Ritter et al. defined face-to-face (F2F) courses as courses which students attended in person with little or no online work. Hybrid courses were defined as classes which had both online and

F2F components with F2F being less than 50% of overall class time. Online courses were conducted exclusively online. Sense of community in each of the three learning environments was measured using the Classroom Community Scale (CCS). The findings of Ritter et al.'s study revealed statistically significant differences between the three learning environments on the overall sense of community ($F = 7.79$, $p < 0.001$) scale and the connectedness sub-scale ($F = 15.28$, $p < 0.000$). There was no statistically significant difference of the learning sub-scale *for* any of the three learning environments ($F = 1.46$, $p < 0.236$). Ritter et al. speculated the reason for the lack of statistical differences on the learning sub-scale may have been due to the fact that all participants were graduate students. Each graduate student was responsible for his or her own learning regardless of the learning environment. The findings further revealed there was statistically significant difference between the F2F ($M = 3.04$, $SD = 0.55$) and hybrid courses ($M = 3.04$, $SD = 0.60$) in the area of *connectedness* when compared to the online courses. This finding was consistent with other research (Rovai & Jordan, 2004). Overall, Ritter et al. (2010) found the majority of participants did experience to some extent a positive sense of *community, connectedness,* and *learning* in all three learning environments (online, hybrid, and F2F) as measured by the CCS (Rovai, 2002).

The findings of Ritter et al.'s study also found a greater sense of community in F2F and hybrid courses than online courses. Results were consistent with findings from Rovai and Jordan (2004). Researchers from both studies (Ritter et al., 2010; Rovai & Jordan, 2004) suggest a key factor in building a sense of community is interaction. Both F2F and blended courses provide opportunites to communicate to other students and with their instructors.

Summary

The literature has shown the importance of interaction in the online learning environment and the impact it has on students' perceived sense of community. A sense of connectedness and shared values among students allows them to actively pursue knowledge in the online learning environment and achieve academic success. Swan (2002, 2003) indicated student-teacher interactions significantly affect learning both in the traditional, face-to-face classroom, and online. Regardless of the learning environment, collaborative learning encourages each student to ask questions, explain and justify their opinions, articulate their reasoning, and elaborate and reflect upon their knowledge (Soller, 2001). Essentially, a key element in building a sense of community is interaction, particularly in online learning environments

(McInnerney & Roberts, 2008; Overbaugh & Nickel, 2010; Swan 2002, 2003).

The theoretical foundation for this study was social constructivism, which emphasizes how social interactions enhance the learning process. Learning is primarily a social product through students' conversation with others, sharing their background information and participating in the give and take of collaborative and cooperative activities (Sthapornnanon, Sakulbumrungsil, Theeraroungchaisri & Watcharadamrongkun, 2009). Students who feel isolated and alienated in their courses due to lack of interaction with their teachers and other students may lack a sense of classroom community (Rovai & Wighting, 2005).

Past research has revealed sense of community has a profound influence on a student's learning experiences (Dawson, 2006; Liu, Magjuka, Bonk, & Lee, 2007). There is specific research which reveals sense of community is gained through interaction and collaboration among the learners, and plays a significant role in promoting a successful online learning experience among graduate students (Dawson, 2006, 2008; Liu et al., 2007; Rovai, 2002; Rovai & Jordan, 2004). Sense of community can be seen when students join together in a particular course or goal (Rovai & Wighting, 2005). By understanding how sense of community impacts student success in an online course, community colleges can develop and design online courses that will meet the needs of its community members. Sense of community contributes to students' motivation, increases learning, reduces feelings' of isolation, and increases retention (Boston, Diaz, Gibson, Ice, Richardson, & Swan, 2009; Shen, Nuankhieo, Amelung, & Laffey, 2008; Wighting, Liu, & Rovai, 2008).

With many students turning to online courses as an alternative method for obtaining a college degree because of the economic issues, family, and work demands many face, there is a demand for online courses. Online education has become very popular in recent years due to its flexibility that allows access to course content anytime and anywhere (O'Lawrence, 2007). Online education allows students to continue their education without interfering with job and career paths. This research explored how the students in two undergraduate community colleges perceive sense of community for students taking online courses compared to those students in traditional courses. Chapter 3 discusses the research design and the research questions that drove this study. Chapter 4 presents the data analysis, and Chapter 5 includes a discussion of the study results. In Chapter 5, it conveys how the results related to the existing body of knowledge and addresses implications for social change, the benefits for online educators, and recommendations for future research.

Chapter 3: Research Method

Introduction

The purpose of this study was to investigate whether traditional and non-traditional age students taking online, blended, and traditional land-based courses differ in their levels of sense of community. The research question guiding this study was, "how do traditional versus non-traditional students at a rural community college compare in their sense of community?"

The purpose of this chapter was to explain the data collection and analysis methodology. The first section details the research design and the research questions. The second section detailed setting, participants, instrumentation and materials, and data collection used for this study. The third section detailed suitability and justification of selection of statistical procedures used to analyze the data. The data analysis included analysis of variance to test the null hypotheses for this study. The fourth section detailed the ethical protection of the participants. The chapter concludes with a summary of the research method and participants used for this study.

Research Design

This non-experimental, quantitative study used a survey methodology to examine student perceptions of sense of community in online courses. Specifically, this research study examined the sense of community among traditional and non-traditional age undergraduate students enrolled in online and traditional learning environments. Independent variables in the study were not manipulated, a control or comparison group was not used, and there was not a random assignment of participant to groups. In addition, non-experimental designs are frequently used in research to describe current existing characteristics such as attitudes, perceptions, values, etc. (Trochim, 2006). Therefore, this study was a non-experimental design.

The dependent variable was sense of community as reflected by scores on the CCS. The independent variables were student status (traditional or non-traditional) and learning environments (online and traditional land-based courses). Traditional students were defined as being students who are between the ages between 18 and 23 (NCES, 2002). Non-traditional students were defined as being students who are 24 years old or older.

Quantitative research is appropriate when "the researcher is testing objective theories by examining the relationship among variables ... so numbered data can be analyzed using statistical procedures" (Creswell, 2009, p. 4). According to Creswell, survey research allows one to generalize information from a sample to a population in order to make inferences about certain characteristics of the population. For this research study, using survey research allowed the researcher to gain a deeper understanding of sense of community for community college students who take online courses. Using an online survey tool such as Survey Monkey, allowed the researcher to re-create the CCS on a secure web-based site. Survey Monkey generated the results in a report for the researcher to download into a spreadsheet or a database for further analysis using SPSS.

The researcher used a survey methodology to collect data. Surveys do, however, have advantages and disadvantages. For example, some advantages to using the survey are that it is an economical and efficient way of collecting data (Creswell, 2009). The cost for Internet-based surveys is lower compared to those administered via the mail. The researcher used a free online survey tool (www.surveymonkey.com) to reproduce Rovai's (2002) Classroom Community Scale in order to distribute the survey to the participants online. The online survey tool, *Survey Monkey*, was at no cost for its basic features such as ten questions per survey and 100 responses per survey;

an easy-to-use web-based survey tool; and able to collect data via web-link, e-mail, Facebook, or embed on one's site or blog. Surveys enable the collection of large amount of data in a short period of time. Another advantage of using survey research is the rapid turnaround time in collecting data from the participants (Creswell, 2009). Other advantages of using the survey are its ability to gather attitudes, values, beliefs, and motives of the respondents (Robson, 2002). Surveys allow respondents to be anonymous, which may encourage frankness if sensitive issues are involved (Robson, 2002). Respondents may decline to participate in surveys because they may be worried their identities will be known and responses will be affixed to each other. The participants may perceive their responses as negative or cynical if they are too forthright. Therefore, when surveys allow respondents to be anonymous, the responses tend to be truer based on their beliefs and attitudes.

Some disadvantages of using surveys are the data may be influenced by respondent's characteristics such as memory, knowledge, experience, motivation, and personality (Robson, 2002). Some respondents may not understand a specific question as it is written on the survey. The researcher did not have the opportunity to clarify the meanings of the questions if the respondent is confused by a certain question. One source of concern is if non-response error(s) occurs (Dillman, Smyth, & Christian, 2009). Dillman et al. (2009) point out a non-response error is when people are selected for the survey, but the participants do not respond. When respondents do not answer a question, the non-responses increase potential for bias. Response bias reduces the probability the data will be valid and generalizable to the target population (Robson, 2002).

Although, the population the researcher surveyed is familiar with taking courses online, they may not be familiar with completing Web-based surveys. Thus, specific instructions were given on how to access and complete the survey (Dillman et al., 2009). This potential area of concern was addressed in the initial e-mail sent to the students in the instructions of how to complete the survey.

This quantitative survey design was appropriate for this research study because the researcher attempted to gather quantitative data on community college students and their perceived sense of community via objective measures of sense of community. A qualitative or mixed-methods designs was not appropriate for this research study because the researcher was not attempting to gather personal experiences of community college students in either type of learning environment: online, hybrid, or traditional land-based learning environments. A non-experimental approach was selected as the researcher did not manipulate any independent variables (Robson, 2002). The researcher did not examine a cause-and-effect relationship between the type of learning environment and sense of community.

Setting

This study examined sense of community among traditional and non-traditional age undergraduate students enrolled in online, blended, and traditional learning environments in two rural community colleges in Maine. The first community college is located in section of rural Maine which is approximately five minutes from the Canadian border. The median income of residents in the community is $31,856 (U. S. Census Bureau, 2010). The primary employment industry in the area is fishing, which results in a low socio-economic status for the residents. The second community college is located in Aroostook County in Presque Isle, Maine.

According to the U. S. Census Bureau (2010), Washington County has approximately 31,000 residents with a median income of $31,856. The per capita income ($14,119) in this county is 20% below the poverty level, compared to Maine's overall poverty level of 12.6%. The data Census data reveals a significant number of citizens have received a high school diploma (79.9%) and the percentage of citizens with a bachelor's degree or higher is 14.7%. Many residents do not continue their education past high school.

According to the U. S. Census Bureau (2010), Aroostook County has approximately 71,000 residents with a median income of $36,574. The per capita income ($20,251) in this county is 15.4% below the poverty level, compared to Maine's overall poverty level of 12.6%. The data Census data reveals that a significant number of citizens have received a high school diploma (83.9%) and the percentage of citizens with a bachelor's degree or higher is 16.2%.

The community colleges where this study was conducted are 2-year institutions regionally accredited by the New England Association of Schools and Colleges, through the Commission on Institutions of Higher Education. One college has an average enrollment of 320 students per semester (WCCC, 2010). Seventy-three percent of the students are full-time and 27% are part-time. Sixty-two percent of the students are age 24 or younger, while 36% are 25 and older based on demographic data from the fall semester of 2008 students' evaluations (WCCC, 2010), while the second college has over 2,000 students registered annually (Northern Maine Community College, n.d.).

Sample

Cohen (1992) stressed the importance of determining the statistical power of a statistical test to determine the suitable sample size for a study. The sample should consist of a minimum of 21 participants for each of the three learning environments (traditional-land based, hybrid, and online) for an overall total sample size of a minimum of 63 participants. Initially the sample size was based on a power analysis using Cohen's *d* (1992). The actual sample consisted of 86 participants (56 participants were traditional-land-based and 30 had some form of online experience). The generally accepted value for power is .80 (80%), with a medium effect size of .14.

Sampling Method/Frame

A purposive sampling method used to recruit participants for the study. According to Robson (2002), a purposive sample is used when, "… the researcher has to achieve a particular purpose" (p. 264). Rather than gathering a random sample of the students enrolled in 2-year institutions, a purposive sample of students from one 2-year institution enrolled in any degree based online, blended, or traditional built learning environment, were used to examine the students' perception of sense of community The inclusion criteria for the study were any student currently enrolled in the college, either in an online, hybrid, or traditional classroom course. Any participant under the age of 18 was excluded from the study. Any student under the age of 18 is considered a child for purposes of this study. According to the National Institute of Health (NIH), children are considered a vulnerable population, and are unable to provide legal effective informed consent: as required by the U. S. Department of Health and Human Services (HHS, 2009) regulations at 45 CFR 46. 116.

The sampling frame of the study were students enrolled at two community colleges. For this research study, the accessible sampling frame was students enrolled either full-time or part-time in an online, blended, or traditional land-based course. The sample frame was from a mix of men and women enrolled in either a certificate program or in an associate's degree program. The age range was from 18 to 100 with a possible mix of ethnic and cultrural backgrounds. Those participants that did not fit the sampling frame were excluded from the study. For example, any student 17 or younger was excluded from the study. As a final point, participants had the right to remove themselves from the study at any time.

Research Questions

The study explored whether there were statistical differences in the sense of community among traditional and non-traditional age undergraduate students enrolled in online, hybrid, and traditional learning environments. The specific research questions included are:

1. What is the difference in overall perceived sense of community for students taking online, hybrid, and traditional land-based courses?

   H_O: There is no statistically significant difference in overall perceived sense of community, as measured by the CCS, for community college students taking online, hybrid, and traditional land-based courses.

   H_A: There is a statistically significant difference in overall perceived sense of community, as measured by the CCS, for community college students taking online, hybrid, and traditional land-based courses.

2. How does traditional and non-traditional student status affect sense of community between traditional and non-traditional students in a rural community college?

   H_O: There is no statistically significant difference in overall perceived sense of community, as measured by the CCS, between traditional and non-traditional age students.

H_A: There is a statistically significant difference in overall perceived sense of community, as measured by the CCS, between traditional and non-traditional age students.

3. How does student status (traditional versus non-traditional) and type of learning environment (online and traditional land based) interact to impact the sense of community for students in a rural community college?

H_O: Student status (traditional versus non-traditional) and type of learning environment (online and traditional land based) do not interact to produce a statistically significant difference in the sense of community for students in a rural community college.

H_A: Student status (traditional versus non-traditional) and type of learning environment (online and traditional land based) do interact to produce a statistically significant difference in the sense of community for students in a rural community college.

Data Collection

Instrumentation and Materials

The Classroom Community Scale (CCS) was used to collect data regarding students' sense of community (Rovai, 2002). Rovai (2002) developed the 20-item CCS to examine sense of community of students within the classroom. The CCS was reproduced using Survey Monkey (http://www.survey.monkey.com), an online survey tool. Written permission to use the CCS was granted by Dr. Alfred Rovai (see Appendix C). The normative sample for the CCS was comprised of 375 students enrolled in 28 different graduate courses via the Blackboard e-learning system from a private university in an urban community (Rovai, 2002).

Scoring the CCS

Three sets of scores were calculated from data obtained by the CCS. The first score was the total score for *classroom community*. The score for classroom community was calculated by adding points assigned to each of the 20 questions in the CCS. Each participant responded to items on the survey using a five-point Likert scale: 4 = *strongly agree*, 3 = *agree*, 2 = *neutral*, 1 = *disagree*, 0 = *strongly disagree.* The total possible score of the classroom community scale ranged from 0 - 80, with higher scores reflecting a strong sense of community.

Two additional scores were calculated for the sub-scales of *connectedness* and *learning.* The scores for the two sub-scales ranged from 0 – 40. For this study, *connectedness* was referred to a sense of cohesion, spirit, trust, and interdependence among students (Rovai, 2002; Rovai, 2002c; Rovai, Whiting, & Lucking, 2004). The overall score for *connectedness* was calculated by adding the points together for each odd item, for example, items 1, 3, 5, 7, 9, 11, 13, 15, 17, and 19, (Rovai, 2002; Rovai & Jordan, 2004; Rovai, Whiting, & Lucking, 2004).

For this study, *learning* was described as, "… the feelings of community members regarding interaction with each other as they pursue the construction of understanding and degree to which members share values and beliefs concerning the extent to which their educational goals and expectations are being satisfied" (Rovai, 2002, pp. 206-207).

To calculate the *learning* sub-scale score, the scores of the remaining even CCS items (2, 4, 6, 8, 10, 12, 14, 16, 18, and 20) was added together.

Validity and Reliability of CCS

Rovai (2002) asserted the procedures used in the development of the CCS provided high confidence the instrument possessed high content and construct validities. Rovai (2002b) used an expert panel of three university professors who taught educational psychology to validate the CCS. At face value, the CCS appeared to measure what it was intended, *classroom community*. Based on the focus group's feedback the instrument was revised to address usability and comprehension based on cultural misunderstandings from the terminology used in the instrument. The Flesch Reading Ease scale was used to assess the readability index of the CCS. The higher the score on the Flesch Reading Ease scale, the easier it is to understand on a 100-point scale (Rovai, 2002). The CCS had a Flesch Reading Ease score of 68.4. This score means the CCS is easy to understand.

Rovai (2002) conducted a reliability analysis of the CCS during the initial development of the survey. Reliability analyses were conducted using Cronbach's coefficient α and the split-half methods (Rovai, 2002). Cronbach's coefficient α for the overall score for the CCS was .93. The split-half coefficient was .91, indicating excellent reliability (Rovai, 2002). The Cronbach's coefficient α and the split-half coefficient for the sub-scale connectedness of the CCS were both .92, indicating excellent reliability. The Cronbach's coefficient α for the sub-scale learning of the CCS was .87 and the split-half coefficient was .80, indicating good reliability (Rovai, 2002).

Rovai (2002) used factor analysis to assess the construct validity of the CCS. The initial findings were based on the correlation matrix of the CCS items. Factor analysis of the data was conducted using direct oblimin[1] rotation to determine the dimensionality of the construct, classroom community. The factor analysis revealed the 20 items on the CCS were correlated with each other (Rovai, 2002). The Kaiser-Meyer-Olkin measure of sampling adequacy was 0.94. This finding indicated the factor analysis assumption of no multi-collinearity (Rovai, 2002) was upheld for the data collected from the CCS. The two factors were moderately related, $r = .60$, $P < .001$. The factor analysis confirmed the two sub-scales (*connectedness* and *learning*) satisfactorily explained a large portion of the variance in the items of the CCS.

The psychometric properties of the CCS have been well supported from other research using the CCS (Rovai, 2002b; Rovai, 2004; Rovai & Jordan, 2004). Other studies (Dawson, 2006; Rovai, 2002b) have reported similar

---

[1] *Direct oblimin rotation is the standard method when one wishes a non-orthogonal (oblique) solution – that is, one in which the factors are allowed to be correlated.*

measures of reliability and validity for the Classroom Community Scale. Rovai (2002b) examined if a relationship existed between sense of community and cognitive learning in an online learning environment. Factor analysis was used to assess the construct validity of the CCS. "The direct oblimin rotated solution yielded two highly interpretable factors, connectedness and learning" (Rovai, 2002b, p. 325). "The connectedness factor accounted for 42.81% of the item variance, and the learning factor accounted for 11.24% of the item variance" (Rovai, 2002b, p. 325).

Dawson conducted a validity study to determine if he could replicate Rovai's (2002) measure of validity for the instrument. Dawson measured the instrument in three distinct phases to ensure it did measure classroom community. The initial phase used a focus group to evaluate the face and content validity. Each group member was asked to indicate if any of the items were ambiguous or confusing. Based on the feedback from the focus group, the CCS was revised to address the usability and comprehension issues that centered on cultural misunderstandings of terminology in the CCS.

The second phase assessed the construct validity of the CCS consisted by using factor analysis (N=160). The internal consistency estimates of reliability were calculated using Cronbach's coefficient alpha and Guttman slit-half coefficients (Dawson, 2006). The results produced a Cronbach's coefficient α of 0.90. The Guttman split-half coefficients for the CCS was 0.89 (Dawson, 2006). Each analysis indicated excellent reliability and consistency of obtained results. The two sub-scales *connectedness* and *learning*, also demonstrated excellent reliability and consistency. The sub-scale *connectedness* generated a Cronbach's coefficient α of 0.86 and Guttman split-half of 0.85. The sub-scale *learning* generated a Chronbach's coefficient alpha of 0.84, and a Guttman split-half 0.76.

Data Analysis

Several statistical procedures were conducted on the data obtained from the participants. Data were analyzed using descriptive and inferential statistical testing. The dependent variable was sense of community as reflected by scores on the CCS. The independent variables were student status (traditional or non-traditional) and learning environment (online, hybrid, and traditional land-based courses). Traditional students were categorized as being between the ages of 18 and 23 (NCES, 2002). Non-traditional students were categorized as being 24 years old or older.

Descriptive statistics were used to describe the demographic characteristics of the sample. Demographic data such as age, ethnicity, gender, number of children, and income level, and number of online and hybrid courses were taken to further describe the overall sample to see if it affects the largest sample of community college students. The demographics further described the overall sample of the community college students to generalize to the large population of community college students. Tables were created to display the descriptive statistics.

Before conducting inferential statistics, the researcher checked to be sure the CCS collects reliable data for this group of students. A reliability analysis was used to assess the reliability of the CCS with this sample of participants. The American Psychological Association (1999) requires information regarding reliability must be reported when using surveys to conduct research. Since reliability is a function of scores and not instruments, the reliability of any instrument may vary from sample to sample (Onwuegbuzie & Daniel, 2003). Before conducting additional tests, the reliability for this group of students were checked to ensure the CCS collects reliable data for this group.

Inferential statistics were used to test the null hypothesis for each research question. Specifically, the researcher used a two-way analysis of variance (ANOVA) procedure to compare the effect of multiple levels of two independent variables. A two-way ANOVA evaluated the main effects and interaction effect between the two independent variables (student status and learning environments). Before running that two-way ANOVA procedure, the researcher tested the statistical assumptions associated with this procedure.

The ANOVA procedure consists of a family of parametric, statistical procedures that are predicated upon several assumptions. The assumptions for the two-way ANOVA are: interval or ratio scale of measurement for the dependent variable, equal sample sizes, independence, normality, and homogeneity (Howell, 2004). These assumptions must be met because they affect the proper use and interpretations of results from a given ANOVA procedure (Mertler & Vanatta, 2005). Therefore, researchers must assess the degree assumptions are met before conducting statistical tests and analyzing the results of such tests (Howell; Mertler & Vanatta).

The scale of measurement assumption posits that data collected for the dependent variable must be at a specific level (Howell, 2004). The dependent variable in this research which will be scores for sense of community (as measured by the CCS) will be measured on an interval level. The equality of sample size assumption posits the size of each group must be approximately equal. The power of the statistical procedure is greatly diminished when sample sizes are disproportionately unequal

(Stevens, 2009). In such cases the research may need to resort to the use of non-parametric statistical procedures such as Freidman's Rank test (Howell). The assumption pertaining to independence states that scores in each sample must be independent and the scores must not be highly correlated with each other (Mertler & Vanatta, 2005). The researcher used the Durbin Watson test to assess the degree of correlation among the variables of interest. The normality assumption posits the patterns of scores for each group should reflect the shape of the normal distribution. The Kilmogorov-Smirnoff and Shapiro-Wilks test statistics was used to test this assumption (Kilpatrick & Feeney, 2007). The homogeneity of variance assumption assumes there is equal variance between groups. The Levene test statistic was used to test this assumption (Kilpatrick & Sweeney). If violations of the assumptions are noted, actions would be taken to address the assumptions. The researcher also provided a discussion of how the assumptions affect the interpretations of data generated for the study.

All data was analyzed using SPSS 18.0 statistical software for analysis. This software was loaded onto the researcher's home computer where the data was stored and analyzed. Missing data, not able to be interpreted from the CCS, was filtered or identified and converted to SPSS as missing data, which was identified by a single period in

SPSS. If a respondent did not answer a question on the survey, the analysis did not provide accurate results. Any uninterruptable data was handled using the "Excluded Cases Pairwise" feature in SPSS. When data was excluded from the calculations, the data provided a more accurate view of the scores on the CCS (George & Mallery, 2007).

Protection of Participants

Ethical considerations are vital to any research endeavor. The researcher complied with the ethical standards of the American Psychological Association. The researcher made efforts to protect the participants who volunteered for the study. The potential risk related to this study were minimal and did not involve premeditated disclosure of confidential information from the survey. The researcher did not contact participants nor collect research data until approval was received from Walden University's Institutional Review Board (IRB) to begin. A letter of cooperation (see Appendix A) from Washington County Community College has been provided as part of the IRB Application. Upon IRB approval, the researcher began soliciting for participants, arranging and distributing surveys, and collecting data.

Participant confidentiality was maintained throughout the study. Data containing personal information such as names, student identification numbers, and e-mail addresses were not collected. Students were e-mailed an invitation letter (see Appendix B) with a link to the web-based version of the CCS. As an adjunct faculty member of the community college, the researcher had access to the college e-mail system and e-mail accounts. The procedures for maintaining confidentiality and anonymity are as follows. The students were informed their participation was voluntary and there was no impact on their course grade(s) or academic standing at the college. Once the data was received, it was stored in an electronic format on a password protected computer at the researcher's home. The specific files containing data were password protected. The computer had restricted access to only the researcher. The researcher was the only one with access and knowledge of the passwords to the data.

Upon collection, analysis, and interpretation of the data, all information will be stored for a minimum of five years in password protected files in the researcher's home. After five years, the data and any information pertaining to the study will be deleted from the computer. Data will be initially deleted from the folders and permanently deleted from the hard drive using disk cleanup. Disk cleanup removes temporary files, empties the recycle bin, and removes a variety of system files and other items no longer needed (available through the Windows file utility).

The results of the study will be shared with community college. As the community college expands their online courses, this knowledge has the potential to aid the college in catching up with the growing trends of online education (Allen & Seaman, 2010). The researcher informed the participants of this in the consent form.

All data collected during the study was checked by the researcher numerous times to ensure accuracy of the findings using the data analysis option provided by Survey Monkey. The researcher exported the data results into SPSS in order to perform further statistically analysis. The researcher provided honest and accurate results in the formal reporting and sharing of the findings.

Informed Consent Protocols

All participants in the study were volunteers. An e-mail was sent to the entire student body at the community college asking if they would like to participate in a research study (see Appendix B). The e-mail contained details of the study, and it outlined any risks and benefits of the study. Directions to accessing and completing the online survey at Survey Monkey, an online survey tool, were provided in the e-mail (see Appendix B). The consent form (see Appendix D) was on the first page of the survey stating the purpose of this study. The student either clicked on "I Agree" or "I

Disagree" with participating or not participating in the study. If the participant agreed to participate in the study, the page automatically moved into the survey questions. If the participant did not agree a "thank you" message appeared and the survey closed. The flow of the pages of the online survey using Survey Monkey, were as follows:

Page 1 – Consent Form – *required*
Page 2 – Demographic Questionnaire
Page 3 – Classroom Community Scale

The second page asked demographic information such as: age, gender, ethnicity, full-time student (at least 4, 3-credit courses), part-time student (3 or less 3-credit courses), employment status, marital status, number of children, level of education completed, income level, and how many online, blended, or traditional land-based learning courses previously taken. The third page consisted of the Classroom Community Scale (see Appendix E for the full set of survey questions).

The security protocols for Survey Monkey, the website hosting the survey were, as follows: the URL of the researcher's survey contained "https://" at the start, so the survey responses are sent over a *secure*, encrypted connection. Survey Monkey maintained a level of encryption: Verisign certificate Version 3, 128-bit encryption. A secure web link was provided in the e-mail invitation (see Appendix B) to restrict access to the survey.

Summary

Using a non-experimental quantitative study, the researcher utilized survey research data to examine the students' sense of community for students' enrolled in an online, blended, and traditional land-based learning environment from two rural Maine community colleges. A web-based survey tool was used to disseminate the Classroom Community Scale to students. The sample consisted of 86 participants of the three learning environments (traditional-land based, hybrid, and online). The assessment tool used was the CCS, which is determined to be psychometrically sound. Data was collected using a secure and encrypted website, with participants guided to the website through an e-mail invitation.

Data integrity and protection of participants was foremost for the researcher throughout the research study. The data was analyzed using SPSS statistical software and a two-way ANOVA analysis to test the hypotheses of the study. The sample size was determined through power analysis using Cohen's d (Cohen, 1992).

There is minimal evidence that explores sense of

community among rural community college students. The numbers of online courses as for both 2- and 4-year institutions are growing. This research study examined how the students in an undergraduate online, hybrid, and traditional land-based learning environment perceive sense of community. To address the gap in the literature, this study sought to explore students' sense of community of rural community college students. This study also explored the relationship of age has to sense of community.

Chapter 4 will present the data analysis and results of the study and Chapter 5 will include a discussion of the study results. In Chapter 5, the researcher will convey how the results relate to the existing body of knowledge and address implications for social change, the benefits for online educators, and recommendations for future research.

Chapter 4: Results

Introduction

The study investigated how sense of community differed among traditional and non-traditional age students enrolled in online, blended, and traditional land-based environments. The research question which guided this study was, "how do traditional versus non-traditional students at a rural community college compare in their sense of community?" This chapter describes the data obtained from the Classroom Community Scale Survey and reports the results of the statistical tests utilized to test the hypotheses for this study.

The first section, a summary of descriptive statistics, presents a summary of frequency counts for the demographic variables, which included age, gender, ethnicity, type of course enrolled, and number of courses enrolled. The next section presented results from the reliability analysis for scores obtained from the CCS. The subsequent section summarizes results from the tests of statistical assumptions for the ANOVA procedure, which consisted of the following: interval or ratio scale of measurement for the dependent variable, equal sample sizes, independence of scores, linearity, normality, and homogeneity of variance (Howell, 2004). Inferential statistics were used to test the null hypotheses for each of the research questions. All statistical analyses were performed using SPSS 18.0 statistical software. The chapter will conclude with a summary of the results from the data analysis.

Preliminary Data Analysis

The initial data analysis consisted of descriptive statistics for the demographic variables (e.g., age, gender, ethnicity). The section also presents a summary of descriptive statistics for the independent variables (type and number of courses currently enrolled in). The details of the preliminary data analyses are reported in the following section.

Description of the Sample

Data was collected from students enrolled in a 2-year degree program from two rural community colleges in Maine. The inclusion criterion for the study was any student who was 18 years or older and currently enrolled in the colleges either in an online, hybrid, or traditional classroom course. A total of 87 college students participated in the study by completing the survey. The age of the targeted sample of participants was between 18-100. Participants who did not meet the inclusion criteria were excluded from the study. Of the 87 participants who volunteered to participate, one participant selected the option for 17 years of age and therefore did not fit the inclusion critieria for the study. Therefore, this participant was excluded from the study and data analysis. The responses for this individual were excluded from the study thus reducing the sample by one (N = 86). Table 1 presents a summary of the demographic data for the participants.

Table 1 Descriptive Data for Traditional and Non-traditional Participants

Age				
	n	%	Valid %	Cumulative %
18-22 years	27	31.4	31.4	32.4
23-30 years	20	23.3	23.3	54.7
31-40 years	24	27.9	27.9	82.6
40 years and up	15	17.4	17.4	100.0
Total	86	100.0	100.0	
Gender				
Male	28	32.6	32.6	32.6
Female	58	67.4	67.4	100.0
Total	86	100.0	100.0	
Ethnicity				
White	71	82.6	82.6	82.6
Asian decent	2	2.3	2.3	84.9
Native American	11	12.8	12.8	97.7
Would rather not say	2	2.3	2.3	100.0
Total	86	100.0	100.0	

Results revealed the majority of participants (31%) were between 18-22 years of age. The smallest number of participants indicated they were over 40 years of age (17.2%). For the purpose of this study, the age of the participants was collapsed into two groups because the study focused on traditional-aged and non-traditional aged students.

The grouping of the two groups was based on prior definitions of what constitutes traditional and non-traditional-aged students. The first group consisted of 27 traditional-aged participants (31.4%). Traditional students were categorized as being between the ages of 18 and 23 (NCES, 2002). The second group consisted of 59 non-traditional-aged participants (68.6%). Non-traditional students were categorized as being 24 years old or older (NCES, 2002).

The majority of participants were female (67.4%). Regarding ethnicity, almost 83% of participants indicated they were White. An equal number of participants selected Asian and Would Rather not say as their ethnic group affiliation.

Table 2 presents frequency counts for the number of students enrolled in each of the types of courses.

Table 2 - Summary Descriptive Data for Course Type, Number of Courses Currently Enrolled, and number of online Courses Taken

	n	%	Valid %	Cumulative %
Type of Courses Currently Enrolled				
Traditional	56	64.4	65.1	65.1
Online	3	3.4	3.5	68.6
Online & Face-to-Face	20	23.3	23.5	92.9
Online & Blended	5	5.8	5.9	98.8
Blended ONLY	1	1.2	1.2	100.0
Total	85	98.8	100.0	
Missing System	1	1.2		
Total	86	100.0		
Number of Courses Enrolled In				
Full-time (3+ courses)	74	86.0	87.1	87.1
Part-time (1-2 courses)	11	12.8	12.9	100.0
Total	85	98.8	100.0	
Missing System	1	1.2		
Total	86			100
Number of Previous Online (OL) Courses				
1-2 OL	42	48.3	56.8	58.1
3-4 OL	18	20.7	24.3	82.4
5 or more	13	14.9	17.6	100.0
Total	73	85.1	100.0	
Missing System	13	14.9		
Total	86	100.0		

The apriori sample size determination revealed a minimum of 21 participants was needed for each of the three learning environments (traditional-land based, hybrid, and online) in order to achieve to maintain the conventional power of .80 for the ANOVA procedure. Therefore, the minimum sample size for an optimum power analysis was 63 participants (Lipsey & Wilson, 1993). Results show while the overall minimum sample size was achieved, the minimum number of participants for each group was not. Consequently, a meaningful comparison could not be made between each of the three learning environments. Due to the small numbers of participants enrolled in two of the learning environments (online and online/blended) the data was collapsed into two categories of courses. The category of traditional enrolled courses (F2F) was retained.

All remaining categories which consisted of some form of online enrollment were collapsed into a single category. That category was named online course (OL). There were 56 participants in the traditional courses and 30 participants in the online courses. The data in Table 2 revealed that over 87% of the participants indicated they were full time students based on the number of courses they were taking. Results further revealed approximately 85% of participants indicated they had taken at least one online course.

Reliability of the CCS

Survey research requires that researchers report information about the reliability of a survey for the sample of participants included in a study (Trochim & Dunnelly,

2007). Reliability is key psychometric property that must be reported because reliability is a function of scores obtained by an instrument and scores gathered by an instrument can vary from sample to sample (Kaplan & Saccuzzo, 2009; Mertler & Vanatta, 2005). The statistical procedures known as reliability and item analyses can be used to measure the psychometric properties of a questionnaire. Cronbach's coefficient alpha (α) was used to measure the internal consistency of the scales included in the CCS (Trochim & Donelly). The significance of the obtained alphas was tested against the value of $\alpha = .70$, because research indicates that values of .70 or greater indicates a reliable scale (Kaplan & Saccuzzo; Mertler & Vanatta).

Table 3 presents a summary of results from the reliability analysis. Results from the reliability analysis generated a Cronbach's $\alpha = .89$ for the overall scale, .84 for the Connectedness Sub-scale, and .86 for the Learning Sub-scale. Each of the three obtained alphas were significantly different from the test value of $\alpha = .70$. Therefore, the sub-scales were deemed to have collected reliable data for the participants in the study.

Table 3 Summary of Reliability Analysis for the Overall Scale and Sub-scale Scores of the CCS

	α	95% Confidence Interval		F Test with True Value .7			
		Lower Bound	Upper Bound	Value	df1	df2	Sig
Connect-edness	.85	.79	.89	1.96	71	711	.000
Learning	.87	.82	.91	2.23	78	702	.000
Overall Scale	.89	.85	.92	2.72	78	1482	.000

The item analysis was conducted by investigating the item-total correlation for items on each scale of the CCS with all other items on the relevant scale. Items with a correlation of .30 or higher were retained for inclusion in subsequent analytic procedures. This value was chosen because it represents the critical value of r with alpha set at .01 and $df = 100$ (Ary, Jacobs, & Razavieh, 1996). Items with lower correlations were excluded from subsequent statistical procedures. Results from the item analysis revealed the total-item correlations ranged from .3 - .677. The results showed the items were internally consistent for the scores obtained in this sample.

Assumption Testing

The two-way ANOVA was used to test the null hypotheses for the research question. The ANOVA procedure consists of a family of parametric, statistical procedures that are predicated upon several assumptions. The assumptions for the two-way ANOVA are: interval or ratio scale of measurement for the dependent variable, equal sample sizes, independence of scores, linearity, normality, and homogeneity of variance (Howell, 2004). These assumptions must be tested because they affect the proper interpretations of results from a given ANOVA procedure (Mertler & Vanatta, 2005).

The ANOVA procedure requires data for the dependent variable be at the interval or ratio level (Stephens, 2009). The dependent variables in the study were scores on the Connectedness and Sense of Community Sub-scales of the CCS. Scores on each sub-scale could range from 0-40, and the scores were measured on the interval level. Therefore, the requirement for this assumption was upheld.

The independence assumption states that scores in each sample must be independent and the scores must not be highly correlated with each other ($r \geq .80$) (Mertler & Vanatta, 2005). It was assumed participants in the sample took the CCS independently online and therefore scores for one participant would not affect the scores of other participants. Results from a correlation analysis also revealed the correlation ($r = .48$, p $= .00$) between the two sub-scales was statistically significant, however the correlation did not exceed the .80 threshold, therefore the requirement of this assumption was met.

The linearity and normality assumptions can be tested at the same time by looking at the distribution of scores on a graph (Mertler & Vanatta, 2005). One graph is the Normal P-P Plot of the Regression Standardized Residuals, which compares the shape of a distribution of scores to the shape of the normal distribution. The shape of the normal distribution is represented by a 45° straight line. When data for a variable is normally distributed, the data on the P-P plot would form a straight 45° line. When the linearity assumption is upheld, the spread of scores would cluster closely to the 45° straight line. Figure 1 shows the P-P Plot for overall scores on the CCS. The two sub-scales (connectedness and learning) are shown in Figures 2 and 3. The graphs reveal the shape of the data points on each of the graphs approximate a straight line and the scores are closely clustered about the line. The assumptions of linearity and normality were upheld for the scores on the CCS for participants in this study.

Normal P-P Plot of Regression Standardized Residual

Dependent Variable: CCS

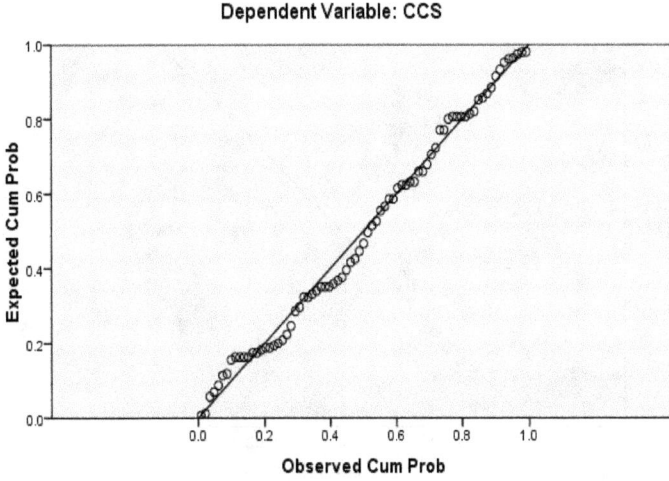

Figure 1 P-P Plot for overall scores on the CCS

Normal P-P Plot of Connectedness

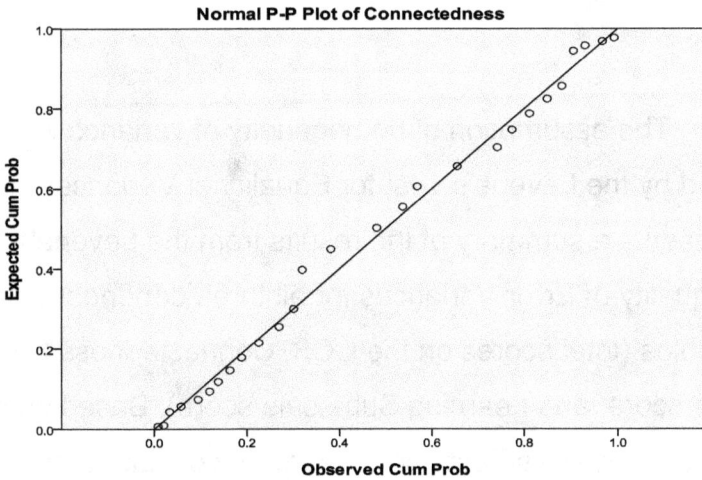

Figure 2 Sub-scale for P-P Plot for overall scores on the CCS

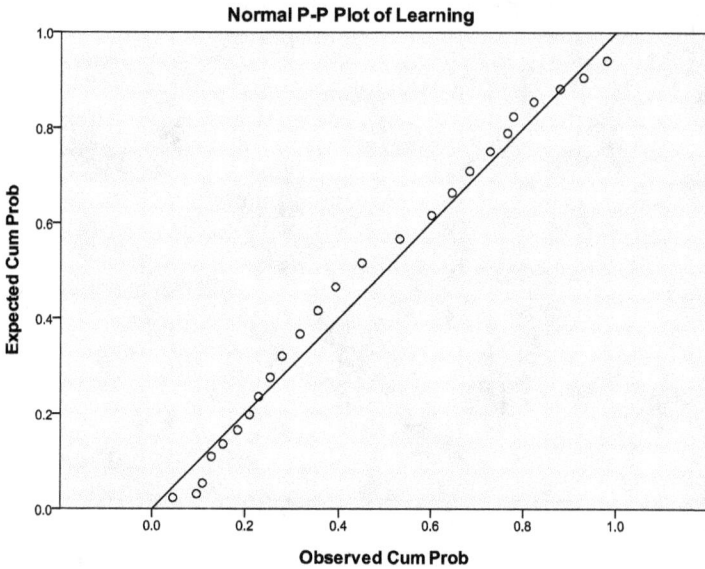

Figure 3 Sub-scale for P-P Plot for overall scores on the CCS

The assumption of homogeneity of variance was tested by the Levene's Test for Equality of Variances. Table 4 presents a summary of the results from the Levene's Test of Equality of Error Variances for all three dependent variables (total scores on the CCS, Connectedness Sub-scale score, and Learning Sub-scale score). Based on data from the Levene's Test, the researcher concluded the variance for group scores on each of the dependent variables was equal. The data from Levene's Test was not significant since each dependent variable had significance greater than .05. The three variances are not significantly different; that is, the three variances are approximately equal. The homogeneity of variance assumption was upheld for this sample of participants.

Table 4 Summary of Levene's Test of Equality for the Overall Scale and Sub-scale Scores of the CCS

Levene's Test of Equality of Error Variances[a]			
Dependent Variable: CCS			
F	df1	df2	Sig.
.243	1	77	.624
Dependent Variable: Learning			
.583	1	77	.447
Dependent Variable: Connectedness			
.655	1	78	.421

Tests the null hypothesis the error variance of the dependent variable is equal across groups.
a. Design: Intercept + Traditional Non-traditional

Main Data Analysis

The data analysis for this study was guided by three main research questions. A two-way ANOVA procedure was used to test the null hypotheses for the research questions. The dependent variable was overall scores on the CCS and the two sub-scales (connectedness and learning). The independent variables were type of courses being taken (traditional face-to-face versus online) and type of student (traditional age versus non-traditional age). Table 5 presents a summary of the ANOVA results for the group differences of the Type of Class (F2F and OL) and student status (traditional-aged and non-traditional aged students). Table 6 presents a summary of the ANOVA results for the overall CCS and sub-scale scores (connectedness and learning) for all three research questions.

Table 5 Summary Table of ANOVA Results for Group Differences of Type of Class and Student Status

Source	df	Mean Square	F	Sig.	η2	Observed Power[b]
Type of class	1	308.858	1.821	0.181	0.024	0.265
status	1	393.806	2.322	0.132	0.031	0.324
Type of class * status	1	730.013	4.304	0.042	0.056	0.535
Error	73	169.623				
Total	77					
Corrected Total	76					

Research Question 1

What is the difference in overall perceived sense of community for students taking traditional land-based course compared to students taking online courses?

H_O: There is no statistically significant difference in overall perceived sense of community, as measured by the CCS, for community college students taking traditional land-based compared to students taking online courses.

H_A: There is a statistically significant difference in overall perceived sense of community, as measured by the CCS, for community college students taking traditional land-based compared to students taking online courses.

Results from the two-way ANOVA are presented in Table 5. The data revealed the test of group differences based on type of class was not statistically significant. The researcher therefore accepted the null hypothesis for Research Question 1 and concluded that sense of community for this sample did not differ for students taking traditional and online courses.

Research Question 2

What is the difference in sense of community for traditional age and non-traditional age students attending a rural community college?

H_O: There is no statistically significant difference in overall perceived sense of community, as measured by the CCS, between traditional and non-traditional age students.

H_A: There is a statistically significant difference in overall perceived sense of community, as measured by the CCS, between traditional and non-traditional age students

Table 5 presents a summary of results from the two-way ANOVA that was used to test the null hypothesis for this research question. The data revealed the test of group differences based on the traditional age students and non-traditional aged students were not statistically significant. The researcher therefore accepted the null hypothesis for Research Question 2.

Research Question 3

How does student status (traditional versus non-traditional) and type of learning environment (traditional land-based courses and online courses) interact to impact the sense of community for students in a rural community college?

H_O: Student status (traditional versus non-traditional) and type of learning environment (traditional land-based courses and online courses) do not interact to produce a statistically significant difference in the sense of community for students in a rural community college.

H_A: Student status (traditional versus non-traditional) and type of learning environment (traditional land-based courses and online courses) do interact to produce a statistically significant difference in the sense of community for students in a rural community college.

Table 5 presents a summary of results from the two-way ANOVA that was used to test the null hypothesis for this research question. The data shows the omnibus F-test of group differences revealed a statistically significant interactive effect (F [1, 73] = 4.30, p = .042). The researcher therefore rejected the null hypothesis for this research question. Table 6 also reveals a small effect size partial η^2 = .07 (Cohen, 1988). The obtained power for the test was .535, which indicated the test was only powerful enough accurately reject the null hypothesis 53.5% of the time. The researcher therefore concluded the results may have been due to chance.

In light of the significant Omnibus test of group scores on the CCS, the researcher conducted a follow-up multivariate ANOVA (MANOVA) on the sub-scale scores of the CCS. The MANOVA procedure is used to test for differences in group scores when there are two or more dependent variables (Mertler & Vanatta, 2005). Table 6 presents a summary of the results. For this analysis the Connectedness and Learning Sub-scale scores were used as the dependent variables. The independent variables were type of class (traditional or online) and student status (traditional age or non-traditional age). Table 6 displays the results for which the data failed to show any statistically significant differences on either of the two dependent variables. There were also no interactive effects between the two variables. The researcher therefore concluded the significant results of Omnibus F- test was due to chance occurrence.

Table 6 Summary Table of MANOVA Results for the Overall CCS and Sub-scale Scores

Source	Dependent Variable	df	Mean Square	F	p	η^2	Observed Power[b]
Type of class	Learning	1	70.894	1.138	0.29	0.015	0.183
	Connected-ness	1	83.805	1.53	0.22	0.021	0.231
status	Learning	1	104.113	1.671	0.2	0.022	0.247
	Connected-ness	1	92.948	1.696	0.197	0.023	0.251
Type of class * status	Learning	1	164.421	2.639	0.109	0.035	0.361
	Connected-ness	1	201.529	3.678	0.059	0.048	0.473
Error	Learning	73	62.312				
	Connected-ness	73	54.79				
Total	Learning	77					
	Connected-ness	77					
Corrected Total	Learning	76					
	Connected-ness	76					

a. R Squared = .037 (Adjusted R Squared = -.002)
b. Computed using alpha = .05
c. R Squared = .049 (Adjusted R Squared = .010)

Summary

The purpose of this research was to determine if there were statistically significant differences in the sense of community among traditional and non-traditional age undergraduate students enrolled in traditionally-land-based and online learning environments. Participants were recruited from two rural community colleges. The independent variables were type of courses being taken (traditional face-to-face versus online) and type of student (traditional age versus non-traditional age). The dependent variables were overall scores on the CCS and the two sub-scales (connectedness and learning). A total of 86 college students participated in the study by completing the survey. The target sample of age of participants was between 18-100. The sample was predominately non-traditional-aged participants (68.6%).

All data was checked prior to data analysis to ensure the statistical assumptions for ANOVA were met. The assumptions were met. Research Question 1 asked what is the difference in overall perceived sense of community for students taking traditional land-based compared to students taking online courses? The results of the two-way ANOVA test for type of class and status revealed the test of group differences based on the students were not statistically significant. The researcher therefore accepted the null hypothesis for Research Question 1.

Research Question 2 asked what is the difference in sense of community for traditional age and non-traditional age students attending a rural community college? The results of the two-way ANOVA test revealed the test of group differences based on the students were not statistically significant. The researcher therefore accepted the null hypothesis for Research Question 2.

Research Question 3 asked how does student status (traditional versus non-traditional) and type of learning environment (traditional land-based courses and online courses) interact to impact the sense of community for students in a rural community college? The results of the two-way ANOVA test revealed the omnibus F-test of group differences revealed a statistically significant interactive effect (F [1, 73] = 4.30, p = .042). The researcher therefore rejected the null hypothesis for this research question. A small effect size was revealed with a partial η^2 = .07 (Cohen, 1988). The obtained power for the test was .535, indicating the test was only powerful enough to reject the null hypothesis 53.5% of the time. The researcher therefore concluded the results may have been due to chance.

Based on the significant interaction effect, a follow-up multivariate ANOVA (MANOVA) analysis for the sub-scale scores of the CCS was performed. The results failed to show any significant differences on either of the two dependent variables. There were not statistically significant interactive effects. The researcher therefore concluded the significant results of Omnibus F- test was due to chance occurrence. Chapter 5 summarizes the results of the findings and discusses the limitations of this study. Chapter 5 furthermore provides suggestions for social change and offers suggestions on recommendations for action and future research.

Chapter 5: Discussion, Conclusions, and Recommendations

Overview

As the United States has transformed from a manufacturing society to a more technology-based, global society, having a college education is more important to an individual's personal success than ever before. According to the U. S. Department of Education (USDE, 2004), earning a college degree leads to benefits for the individual and for the society in which the person lives. Even though there is a documented link between higher wages and having a college degree (Day & Newburger, 2002), it is not easy for everyone to attend college or even to obtain a college degree.

Some students may experience difficulties or impediments that prevent them from attending or completing college. Some of those challenges to getting a college degree are time constraints, distance, and finances (Sherry, 2006). The distance to the nearest college may be at least 50-100 miles away for students in rural communities. Many students also face mounting family responsibilities and job constraints, both of which may interfere with going to college (Miller & Lu, 2002). Online education has allowed many individuals to minimize some of these challenges and to have an opportunity to obtain a college degree. The Internet has become the medium that has provided access for individuals who might not otherwise have the opportunity to earn a college degree.

According to several studies (Allen & Seaman, 2007; Kassop, 2003; McGorry, 2003), flexibility in access is one of the main reasons students take online courses. Consequently, an increasing number of students are opting to take courses online, and the increased demand for online classes has resulted in institutions offering more online courses. Although online classes have increased, research indicates students who take online courses often experience feelings of isolation and loneliness (Rovai & Wighting, 2005). Research by Hawthornthwaite, Kazmer, Robins, and Shoemaker (2000) has shown feelings of isolation are related to a low sense of community for students in online courses. Consequently, as some students experience feelings of isolation, they may eventually drop out of an online course and perhaps drop out of college (Rovai, 2002; Rovai, 2004; Rovai & Wighting, 2005).

Sense of community is defined as "a feeling that members have of belonging, feeling that members matter to one another and to the group, and a shared faith that members' needs will be met through their commitment to be together" (McMillan & Chavis, 1986, p. 9). Sense of community plays a distinct role in students' success in their courses and in college. The building of knowledge results from active social interaction among learners (Rovai & Wighting, 2005). Collaborative activities that facilitate and promote social interaction have the potential for reducing feelings of isolation and increasing sense of community (Rovai & Wighting, 2005).

The student population for most community colleges is usually non-traditional, low-income, and minority students (Provasnik & Planty, 2008). Non-traditional-aged students may have difficulty experiencing sense of community compared to their younger counterparts. The older non-traditional student may not feel as connected to their classmates. This sense of being disconnected from their classmates may cause the non-traditional student to feel he or she is not a member of the learning community (Rovai, Wighting, & Jing, 2005). There is limited research conducted that examines the sense of community by learning environment for community college students in rural areas. Few researchers have examined the sense of community of students taking online courses at rural community colleges.

The purpose of this quantitative, non-experimental study was to examine student perceptions of sense of community in two rural community colleges. The researcher used the survey methodology to collect data that allowed examination of sense of community among traditional and non-traditional students enrolled in online and traditional land-based learning environments at two rural community colleges. The study included data from students who are currently enrolled in undergraduate degree-based programs. The dependent variable were sense of community as reflected by scores on the CCS. The independent variables were student status (traditional or non-traditional) and learning environment (online and traditional land-based courses).

The following three research questions guided this study: What is the difference in overall perceived sense of community for students taking online, hybrid, and traditional land-based courses? How does traditional and non-traditional student status affect sense of community between traditional and non-traditional-age students in a rural community college? How does student status (traditional versus non-traditional) and type of learning environment (online, hybrid, and traditional land based) interact to impact the sense of community for students in a rural community college? This chapter presents an interpretation of the findings relative to previous literature that has been conducted. The findings will be interpreted individually for each research question.

Interpretation of Findings

Research Question 1

The first research question assessed the difference in overall perceived sense of community for students taking traditional land-based courses compared to students taking online courses. The results indicated no significant difference between the groups (type of status) in the students' overall perceived sense of community. Even though there was not a significant difference in the findings, this research does add to the literature.

Findings from the current study differ from findings by Ritter, Polnick, Fink, and Oescher (2010), which found a greater sense of community in the traditional and blended courses than the online courses. Ritter et al. examined three delivery methods (face-to-face, hybrid, and online) to determine if there were differences in how each environment stimulated sense of community among students. The findings of Ritter et al.'s study revealed statistically significant differences between the three learning environments on the overall sense of *community* scale and the *connectedness* sub-scale. The results from

Ritter et al.'s study also revealed there was no statistically significant difference of the learning sub-scale *for* any of the three learning environments. However, this research study did not reveal any significant differences among online or traditional-land-based environments on any of the scales (community, connectedness, and learning). The lack of significance may have been due to each students' prior experience with online learning, which increased their level of community. For example, Table 2 illustrates approximately 85% of participants indicated they had taken at least one online course prior to participating in the study.

Results from this research study were consistent with the findings from Rovai and Jordan's (2004). This researcher's findings were similar to Rovai and Jordan in that there was no statistically significant differences between the student scores on any of the scales (community, connectedness, and learning) for any of the two learning environments (online and traditional-land-based environments). Rovai and Jordan suggested the students' perception of their sense of community for the online courses may have been influenced by how a student learns as well as the student's learning style, self-motivation, interest in the material presented in the course, support from the family, and learner's level of responsibility for their own learning (Irizarry, 2002). The same factors Rovai and Jordan (2004) and Irizarry (2002) suggested may have also influenced this research study's findings as some students' had prior online experience as expressed in Table 2. Also, the interaction in both online and traditional-land-based courses may have provided opportunities for the students to share ideas and experiences, which may have increased their level of community.

Research Question 2

The second research question assessed whether traditional and non-traditional student status affected sense of community among students in a rural community college. The results of this research study indicated no significant difference between any of the groups (type of class: online and traditional-land-based courses) and student status: traditional and non-traditional age).

Results from this research study were also similar from findings of a previous study conducted by Rovai and Jordan (2004). The two researchers examined the differences between perceived sense of community of students enrolled in the traditional classroom, blended learning environment, and a fully online learning environment. Their findings showed students in the online course yielded the lowest marginal mean on the Connectedness Scale of the CCS. The findings lacked significance. The scores of participants in the traditional-land-based course and the scores from the online course were not statistically significant. The researcher's findings did not reveal any statistically significant differences between any of the groups (online or traditional-land based) as demonstrated in Table 6.

Research Question 3

The third research question addressed whether student status (traditional versus non-traditional) and type of learning environment (online, hybrid, and traditional land based) interact sense of community for students in a rural community college?

The results of the study revealed no statistically significant interaction between student status and type of learning environment. The lack of significance may be the result of prior exposure to online learning. For example, Table 2 illustrates approximately 85% of participants indicated they had taken at least one online course prior to participating in the study. The majority of participants in this research study had some exposure to online experience. Forty-two participants (48.3%) had at least one or more online course or some form of online experience.

Results from this research study were not consistent with a previous research. A study conducted by Ritter et al. (2010) found the majority of the participants did experience to some extent a positive sense of *community*, *connectedness*, and *learning* in all three learning environments (online, hybrid, and F2F) when examining sense of community. Statistically significant differences were shown of the perceptions of online students to face-to-face students (Ritter et al.). A greater sense of community was found in the face-to-face classes than in the online classes.

Theoretical Background

The theoretical foundation for this study was social constructivism, which emphasizes how social interactions with others enhance the learning process. Research has shown that optimal learning occurs in a constructivist setting (Jonassen, Peck, & Wilson, 1999; Kasworm, 2003; Vygostky, 1978). Humans are social creatures, and for this reason humans tend to grow and develop through social interactions in a variety of communities (Woo & Reeves, 2007). According to Vygotsky (1978), all cognitive functions such as thinking and problem solving are viewed as products of the interactions of others. The types of interactions in a classroom include discussion with other students and interactions with the teacher.

Learning is primarily a social process. Students' conversations with their classmates allow them to share their backgrounds. Conversations and dialogue allow students to participate in the give and take of collaborative and cooperative activities (Sthapornnanon, Sakulbumrungsil, Theeraroungchaisri, & Watcharadamrongkun, 2009).

The theory of social constructivism has primarily been used for the traditional classroom. However, as online classrooms begin to develop and grow, the principles of constructivism can also be used to explain how sense of community is developed in online and hybrid courses. Redfern and Naughton (2002) stated learning is not achieved as an "isolated individual act, but a collective result of social interaction" (p. 2). In order for this social interaction and learning to occur, a sense of community must be built (Redfern & Naughton, 2002; Rovai & Wighting, 2005; Shea, 2006).

Even though research (Redfern & Naughton, 2002; Rovai & Wighting, 2005; Shea, 2006) has demonstrated social interaction is important in fostering sense of community, my study revealed no statistically significant differences among the two groups (F2F and OL). Also, there was no significant interaction for student status (traditional versus non-traditional) and type of learning environment (online and traditional land based) between sense of community. The data revealed a large portion of students had some form of online experience, which may account for the lack of interaction for the group of students.

According to Schweir and Balbar (2002) and Weasenforth, Biesenbach-Lucas, and Meloni (2002), effective learning communities are founded on social constructivist pedagogy and promote online learning communities. Lee et al. (2006) revealed that 93% of the students reported they strongly agreed or agreed they participated in a constructivist learning environment. The participants reported they had explored, experimented, and engaged in active learning activities that provided them with information they were able to apply to practice.

Swan (2002, 2003) indicated student-teacher interactions significantly affect learning both in the traditional, face-to-face classroom, and online. Regardless of the learning environment, collaborative learning encourages each student to ask questions, explain and justify their opinions, articulate their reasoning, and elaborate and reflect upon their knowledge (Soller, 2001). Essentially, a key element in building a sense of community is interaction, particularly in online learning environments (McInnerney & Roberts, 2008; Overbaugh & Nickel, 2010; Swan 2002, 2003).

With regard to the theoretical foundation for this research study, it is the social interaction, and social context that provides the basis for individuals to gain knowledge and create meaning from social activities. The interaction in both online and traditional-land-based courses of this research study may have provided opportunities for the students to share ideas and experiences, which may have increased their perceived level of sense of community. Rovai and Wighting (2005) suggest that learning occurs most effectively when there is a strong sense of community among its members. The collaborative activities within the learning environments of this research study may have promoted significant social interaction among the students. This interaction may have reduced the students' feelings of isolation and increased their sense of community (Rovai & Wighting, 2005) accounting for the lack of significance in this research study's findings.

Limitations

Limitations for this study were taken into account and include the population from which the sample was taken. The population was limited to undergraduate students enrolled at two sites. This sample may not have been representative of students attending other institutions and courses, thus limiting generalizability and external validity of the findings (Trochim, 2006). For example, the county of one community college in which the college is located in has a population of 32,856 for 2010. In contrast, a southern area in which a community college exists, has a population of 281,674 for 2010 (U. S. Census Bureau, 2011). As such, the findings of this study may not be generalized outside those who participated.

This study focused on undergraduate college students; therefore, the results may or may not be generalizable to graduate students with a higher educational level. It may be assumed graduate students have previous online learning experience, thereby, contributing to a greater sense of community. Rovai (2002c) suggest online graduate students feel connected to their online classroom community. Students with a stronger sense of community tend to possess a greater sense of perceived cognitive learning (Rovai, 2002c). Graduate students may be more responsible for their own learning. Rovai and Jordan (2004) suggest a student's learning style, self-motivation, interest in the material presented in the course, support from family, and learner's level of responsibility for their own learning (Irizarry, 2002) may factor into the degree to which a student experiences a sense of community. Even though Rovai and Jordan (2004) point out many confounding variables that may factor into a students' level of sense of community, this research study's current results cannot be inferred to a broader population such as graduate students with a higher educational level.

The student population for most community colleges

usually consists of non-traditional, low-income, and minority students (Provasnik & Planty, 2008). The sampling frame has defined the target population as those enrolled at two community colleges from which the sample was drawn and to which the sample data was generalized. Therefore, results only reflect the population of undergraduate community college students from which the data was collected. The findings may not be generalizable to a broader population. The findings of this small study may not generalize to other community colleges. There is a need to further investigate the role of sense of community among a larger sample of community college students.

Some other confounding variables that could potentially impact the students' perception of sense of community include instructor teaching style, teaching philosophy, and online teaching experience of the teacher. For example, when teachers initiate dialogue and illustrate course concepts through activities that build essential skills and knowledge for the students, it clarifies concepts and reduces students' confusion (Tsai, 2007). Researchers (Shea, Li, & Pickett, 2006) examining teacher presence in online and class-based learning environments and its influence on students' sense of community found a significant correlation between classroom community and teacher presence. The study found correlations between learning community and teaching presence, instructional design and organization, and directed facilitation were high (Shea et al.). However, the study had no significant difference of teacher presence between the two learning environments, online and class-based, and in the total classroom community. These confounding variables identified by other researchers may have influenced my study and thereby, may be potential limitations.

When the teacher lacks the skills to facilitate and moderate online discussions, this limits the opportunities for collaboration and interaction among the students (Rovai & Downey, 2010). This may limit the opportunities for students to establish sense of community in online classes. Some variables not included in the study were teaching style, teaching philosophy, and online teaching experience of the teacher. There may be fundamental differences in instructional strategies of the course of the teachers, which may impact the class' sense of community.

Another limitation of the study pertains to the use of the self-report survey data. Creswell (2009) suggested some respondents may not have answered the survey questions truthfully. Response bias is the effect of nonresponses on a survey (Creswell). The respondents may have responded to the survey questions based on the assumption of how I wanted them to respond. This is another form of response bias, called social desirability (Lee & Woodliffe, 2010). Social desirability occurs when respondents tend to conform to the actual or perceived social norms in terms of certain values, traits, attitudes, interests, opinions, and behaviors (Lee & Woodliffe). Some respondents also marked neutral answers. Therefore, the data and the results are only valid as the responses to the survey questions are honest and truthful. However, results from the researcher's reliability analysis of the *Classroom Community Scale* generated a Cronbach's α = .89 for the overall scale, .84 for the Connectedness Sub-scale, and .86 for the Learning Sub-scale. Each of the three obtained alphas were significantly different from the test value of α = .70. Therefore, the sub-scales were deemed to have collected reliable data for the participants in the study.

Even though the researcher did collect data on gender and ethnicity, these elements were not examined for how these two variables affected students' level of sense of community. A study examining individual differences in sense of community within a blended learning environment found statistical differences in scores based on gender (Graf, 2003). This is consistent with previous research (Rovai 2001), which pointed out females tend to communicate and interact in learning environments to seek out relations with others and connect with their gender peers, whereas males tend to communicate using a more autonomous and independent communication style (Rovai). This may also be a limitation to the study since the study had more female than male participants. Thus, there was not an equal distribution of female and male participants. This may be a limitation since researchers (Rovai & Baker, 2005) found females felt more connected than their male counterparts when examining gender differences in online learning.

Ethnicity may also have been a factor that affected the results of this study since the demographic data showed a larger number of Caucasian students than any other ethnicity. Previous research (Kawachi, 2003) points out there are cultural differences in learning, such as learning cooperatively-in-a-group or collaboratively-in-a-group. The researcher did not have control over data related to the courses being taught or how the courses were taught, so ethnicity may be a factor affecting the results as well as a possible limitation. The sample did not contain an equal distribution of ethnic backgrounds; thereby suggesting there may be fundamental differences in ethnicity, which may impact the class' sense of community. Researchers (Beil & Shope, 1990) suggest ethnicity influences sense of community. However, there is limited research on the issue of ethnicity and sense of community.

Implications for Social Change

The findings from this study present several potential implications for positive social change. The implication for positive social change includes assisting rural community colleges in developing effective online courses with strategies and activities that promote collaboration and interaction in the hopes of decreasing attrition and promoting retention in online courses. This study may shed some light on the perceptions of the students as to what does or does not foster sense of community because even with some form of online experience students' perceived a sense of community.

Another implication for positive social change includes insight in how sense of community may be fostered in the virtual environment. Rovai (2002c) acknowledged to increase retention of students, faculty, and educational institutions must provide increased support by promoting a strong sense of community. This may be accomplished through establishing strategies that enable students to make connections with other learners. Parloff and Pratt (2007) suggest these strategies for fostering a community in an online learning environment: "promote a sense of autonomy, initiative, and creativity while encouraging questioning, critical thinking, dialogue, and collaboration" (p.40). Sense of community can also be fostered through actions that provide students with a large base of academic support (Rovai, 2002c). In spite of the researcher's findings, no statistically significant differences were found among any of the groups related to classroom community. The researcher's findings do not negate the importance of promoting sense of community as it has the potential for opportunities of having a successful learning experience.

Sense of community may not be much of an issue at these two community colleges as originally assumed. Thus, this research shows these two colleges are doing a better job of working with this variable, *sense of community*. Since a large percentage of community college students fit into the non-traditional category (IES, 2009) with regard to age, this population of college students face many challenges of both work and family responsibilities. These challenges may impede the non-traditional-age students from completing their education. Researchers (Carr, 2000; Terry, 2001) report there is minimal empirical evidence examining retention rates other than from individual academic institutions examining course completion and program retention rates. Through examining the students' experiences and attitudes with regard to sense of community perhaps at several points during their college experience, we can explore how these experiences affect retention. The ultimate goal for any student regardless of age is to have a positive learning experience.

Recommendations for Action

Since online learning lacks the physical social interaction that exists in the traditional classroom, students may experience feelings of being isolated and disconnected. The feelings of isolation and loneliness may lead to a negative learning experience (Outzs, 2006; Rovai & Wighting, 2005). Consequently, the feelings of isolation may lead to some students dropping out of online courses and perhaps dropping out of college (Rovai, 2002; Rovai, 2004; Rovai & Wighting, 2005). In spite of my findings of no statistically significant differences among the groups (online and traditional-land-based environments) to classroom community, it does not negate the importance of promoting sense of community so students have the opportunity for a successful learning experience. Community colleges should have regular continuing education workshops for their instructional designers and faculty focusing on ways to promote sense of community among their students.

Recommendations for Further Study

There is limited research found that specifically examined sense of community at rural community colleges. Research has demonstrated how sense of community contributes to students' motivation, increases learning, reduces feelings' of isolation, and increases retention (Boston, Diaz, Gibson, Ice, Richardson, & Swan, 2009; Shen, Nuankhieo, Amelung, & Laffey, 2008; Wighting, Liu, & Rovai, 2008). Future research might examine rural community colleges and sense of community to determine if or how teaching style or teaching experience is a contributing factor in a students' sense of community. There may be fundamental differences in instructional strategies of the online course instructors, which may impact the students' sense of community in online courses. Future research could examine the relationship of these variables as they relate to classroom community as well as identify course designs and pedagogy that might promote classroom community in various online learning environments (Rovai, 2002b).

Since the Internet has become the medium that allows individuals the opportunity to earn a college degree, students are in part turning to online learning as an alternative to attending traditional classroom based education. As the newness of online courses wears off, online learners may become less tolerant of poor online course experiences (Rovai, 2002b). Further research might examine various instructional strategies in online courses to determine which strategies promote sense of community and provide positive learning experiences.

Even though the researcher's findings are not consistent with previous research, the lack of significant differences on the overall sense of community among the groups as well as the lack of significant interaction among these particular students may warrant further study. For example, 48.8% of the participants had experienced some form of online learning experience or exposure. Future research may also examine the amount of exposure or experience with an online learning environment to determine the level of sense of community.

The researcher's findings revealed almost 83% of participants indicated they were Caucasian. An equal number of participants selected Asian and 'would rather not say' as their ethnic group affiliation. The majority of participants were women (67.4%) and the remaining 32.6% were men. Although the researcher did not specifically examine ethnicity and gender with regard to students' overall sense of classroom community in the research, it is suggested that future research should be directed at identifying collaborative online instructional approaches that encourage a sense of community among culturally diverse students.

The research showed the majority of participants (68.6%) were non-traditional-aged participants while only 31.4% were traditional-age participants. A large percentage of community college students fit into the non-traditional category (IES, 2009). The results of this research study indicated no statistically significant difference between any of the groups (type of class: online and traditional-land-based courses) and (student status: traditional and non-traditional age). Sense of community may not be much of an issue at these two community colleges as originally assumed with regard to age. Research has shown students at different ages learn differently (Miller & Lu, 2003). Future research should be directed at identifying instructional strategies that encourage a sense of community among the non-traditional students that fosters sense of community in both undergraduate and graduate institutions.

Summary

This research study was conducted using a non-experimental quantitative study. An online survey examined the perceptions of students' enrolled in an online and traditional land-based learning environment from two rural community colleges. This research study examined how students in an undergraduate traditional land-based and online learning environment perceive sense of community. In order to address the gap in the literature, this study sought to explore students' sense of community of rural community college students. This study explored the relationship of age and its impact on sense of community.

According to the U. S. Department of Education (USDE, 2004), earning a college degree leads to benefits for the individual and for the society in which the person lives. Cumulatively, the research shows a college education is important not only to the individual, but to society as a whole (Baum & Payea, 2005; Hill et al., 2005). When individuals successfully complete a college degree, the individual increases their earning potential and are more likely to become productive and engaged members of society (Baum & Payea; Hill et al.). As we move further into the 21st century, it is imperative more Americans enter into and graduate from college.

The Bureau of Labor Statistics (2009) has projected almost half of the jobs will be created by 2018 will require a postsecondary education. The BLS (2009) has projected by 2018 the number of occupations that will require a bachelor's degree or higher is expected to be 11.7 million. Therefore, to be competitive in the employment sector, individuals must work toward having a college degree. The data of this study demonstrates students from two rural communities are attempting to obtain a college degree. Even though the findings do not provide any statistical significance with regard to classroom community among class status or learning environment, it does provide the foundation for future examination of these variables on a larger scale.

In spite of the findings of no statistically significant differences among the groups (online and traditional-land-based environments) and student status (traditional age and non-traditional age students) to classroom community and the two sub-scales (*connectedness* and *learning*), researchers have (Ritter, Polnick, Fink, &Oescher, 2010) found a greater sense of community in traditional courses than online courses. Research has consistently revealed interactions between the teacher and the student, as well as the student interactions with their classmates, are crucial to students' online learning (Rovai, 2001; Swan, 2002, 2003; Webb-Boyd, 2008; Woo & Reeves, 2007). Sense of community plays a significant role in promoting a successful learning experience for students (Dawson, 2008; Liu, Magjuka, Bonk, & Lee, 2007; Rovai, 2002; Rovai & Jordan, 2004).

Collectively, research shows encouraging and fostering positive social interactions promotes active learning and enhances the students' sense of community (Rovai, 2007). To increase retention of students, faculty and educational institutions, must provide increased support by promoting a strong sense of community (Rovai 2002c) for their students. As rural community colleges expand online courses and curriculum to meet the growing needs of the community, this study may be the foundation of a larger study in this venture through a larger sample size and having more than two community colleges to draw the data from. Although the findings were not consistent with previous research (Rovai, 2001; Swan, 2002, 2003; Webb-Boyd, 2008; Woo & Reeves, 2007), this study may provide the background for community colleges to gain a better understanding as to the degree to which the different learning environments foster sense of community for its students.

References

Abdous, M , & Yen, C. (2010). A predictive study of learner satisfaction and outcomes in face-to-face, satellite broadcast, and live video-streaming learning environments. *Internet & Higher Education*, 13(4), 248-257. doi:10. 1016/j. iheduc. 2010. 04. 005

Allan, I. E., & Seaman, J. (2003). Seizing the opportunity: The quality and extent of online education in the United States, 2002 and 2003. Retrieved on August 10, 2008, from http://www. sloan-c. org/resources/sizing opportunity. pdf

Allen, I. E., & Seaman, J. (2006). Making the grade: Online education in the United States, 2006. Needham, MA: The Sloan Consortium.

Allen, I. E., & Seaman, J. (2007). *Online nation: Five years of growth in online learning*. Retrieved August 8, 2010, from http://www. sloan-c. org/resources/onlinenation. pdf

Allen, I. E., & Seaman, J. (2010a). Class Differences: Online Education in the United States, 2010. Retrieved August 8, 2010, from http://sloanconsortium. org/publications/survey/class_differences

Allen, I. E., & Seaman, J. (2010b). Learning on demand: Online education in the United Stated, 2009. Retrieved August 8, 2010, from http://www. sloan-c. org/publications/survey/pdf/learningondemand. pdf

Allen, K. (2005). Online learning: constructivism and conversation as an approach to learning. *Innovations in Education & Teaching International*, 42(3), 247-256. doi:10. 1080/01587910500167985

Anderson, T., & Elloumi, F. (Eds.). (2004). Theory and practice of online learning. Retrieved on January 29, 2010, from http://unpan1. un. org/intradoc/groups/public/documents/APCITY/UNPAN017431. pdf

Arbaugh, J. B., & Benbunan-Fich, R. (2007). The importance of participant interaction in online environments. *Decision Support Systems, 43*, 853-865. doi: 10. 1016/j. dss. 2006. 12. 013

Aud, S., Hussar, W., Kena, G., Bianco, K., Frohlich, L., Kemp, J., & Tahan, K. (2011). *The Condition of Education 2011* (NCES 2011-033). U.S. Department of Education, National Center for Education Statistics. Washington, DC: U.S. Government Printing Office.

Bandura, A. (2001). Social Cognitive Theory: An Angetic. *Annual Review of Psychology, 54*(1), 1-26. Retrieved from http://exordio. qfb. umich. mx/archivos%20PDF%20de%20trabajo%20UMSNH/Aphilosofia/2007/Ban duraARP2001r. pdf

Baruch, Y., & Holtom, B. C. (2008). Survey response rate levels and trends in organizational research. *Human Relations, 61*, 1139. doi: 10. 1177/0018726708094863. Retrieved from http://hum. sagepub. com/cgi/content/abstract/61/8/1139

Beil, C., & Shope, J. H. (1990). No exit: Predicting student persistence. *Paper presented at the Annual Forum of the Association for Institutional*

Research. Educational Reproduction Services Number ED 321669.

Benbunan-Fich, R., & Arbaugh, J. B. (2006). Separating the effects of knowledge construction and group collaboration in learning outcomes of web-based courses. *Information & Management, 43*, 778-793. doi: 10. 1016/j. im. 2005. 09. 001

Benshoff, J. M., & Lewis, H. A. (1992). Non-traditional college students. Ann Arbor, MI: ERIC Clearinghouse on Counseling and Personnel Services. Retrieved from ERIC database. (ED3347483)

Beyth-Marom, R., Chajut, E., Roccas, S., & Sagiv, L. (2003). Internet-assisted versus traditional distance learning environments: Factors affecting students' preferences. Computers & Education, 41, 65-76. doi:10. 1016/S0360-1315(03)00026-5

Bocchi, J., Eastman, J. K., & Swift, C. (2004). Retaining the online learner: Profile of students in an online MBA program and implications for teaching them. *Journal of Education for Business, 79*(4), 245-253.

Braveman, P. A., Cubbin, C., Egerter, S., Williams, D. R., & Pamuk, E. (2010). Socioeconomic disparities in health in the United States: What the patterns tell us. *American Journal Of Public Health, 100*(S1), S186-S196. doi:10. 2105/AJPH. 2009. 166082

Bronack, S., Riedl, R , & Tashner, J. (2006). Learning in the zone: A social constructivist framework for distance education in a 3-dimensional virtual world. *Interactive Learning Environments 14*(3), 219-232. Retrieved on August 10, 2008, from EBSCO database.

Bruner, J. S. (1996). *The culture of education*. Cambridge, MA: Harvard University Press.

Bureau of Labor Statistics. (1999). More education: Higher earnings, lower employment. *Occupational Outlook Quarterly*. Retrieved from http://www. bls. gov/opub/ooq/1999/Fall/oochart. pdf

Bureau of Labor Statistics. (2010). Spotlight on statistics: Back to college. Retrieved from http://www. bls. gov/spotlight/2010/college/

Bureau of Labor Statistics. (2011a). Usual weekly earnings of wage and salary workers: Second quarter 2011. Retrieved from http://www. bls. gov/news. release/pdf/wkyeng. pdf

Bureau of Labor Statistics. (2011b). Volunteering in the United States, 2010. Economic News Release. Retrieved from http://www.bls.gov/news.release/volun. r0.htm

Bureau Of Labor Statistics. (2011c). Employment characteristics of families — 2010. News Release. Retrieved from http://www.bls.gov/news.release/archives/famee_03242011.pdf

Burns, M. (Ed.). (1998). Constructivism and technology: On the road to student-centered learning. Southwest Educational Development Laboratory. Tap Assistance Program into Learning, 1. Web: http://www. sedl. org/tap

Bye, D., Pushkar, D., & Conway, M. (2007). Motivation, interest, and positive affect in traditional and non-traditional undergraduate students. *Adult Education Quarterly, 57*(2), 141-158.

Carnevale, D. (2000). Social bonds found to be crucial in online education. *Chronicle of Higher Education, 47*(9), A48. Retrieved from Academic Search Complete database.

Carr, S. (2000). As distance education comes of age, the challenge is keeping the students. *The Chronicle of Higher Education, 46*(23), A39 – A41.

Center for Disease Control and Prevention (2008). A program for early release of selected estimates from the National Health Interview Survey. National Center for Health Statistics. June 2009. Available from: http://www. cdc. gov/nchs/data/nhis/earlyrelease/ER_booklet. pdf

Chickering, A., & Gamson, Z. (1987). Seven principles for good practice in undergraduate education. *American Association of Higher Education Bulletin*, 3–7.

Cohen, J. (1992). A power primer. *Psychological Bulletin, 112*(1), 155-159. Retrieved from EBSCO*host*.

Congressional Research Service. (2004). Cash and non-cash benefits for persons with limited income: Eligibility rule, recipient, and expenditure data, FY 2000-2002. *Congressional Research Service*, Report RL32233. Retrieved from http://assets. opencrs. com/rpts/RL32233_20031125. pdf

Creswell, J. (2009). *Research design, qualitative, quantitative, and mixed methods approaches* (3rd ed.). Los Angeles, CA: Sage.

Crissey, S. R. (2009). *Educational attainment in the United States: 2007.* Current Population Reports. Washington : U. S. Census Bureau. Retrieved from http://www. census. gov/prod/2009pubs/p20-560. pdf

Cross, K. P. (1980, May). Our changing students and their impact on colleges: Prospects for a true learning society. *Phi Delta Kappan*, 630-632. EJ221597

Curtis, D. D., & Lawson, M. J. (2001). Exploring collaborative online learning. Journal of Asynchronous Learning Networks, 5(1), 21-34. Retrieved from http://scholar. googleusercontent. com/scholar?q=cache:UrnltIxAieEJ:scholar. google. com/+benefits+of+online+learning&hl=en&as_sdt=0,20

Czaja, S. J., & Sharit, J. (1993). Age differences in the performance of computer-based work. *Psychology and Aging, 8*(1), 59-67. doi:10. 1037/0882-7974. 8. 1. 59

Dawson, S. (2008). A study of the relationship between student social networks and sense of community. *Educational Technology & Society, 11*(3), 224–238.

Day, G. C., & Newburger, E. C. (2002). T*he big payoff : Educational attainment and synthetic estimates of work-life earnings*. Current Population Reports. Washington, DC: U. S. Census Bureau. Retrieved from http://www. census. gov/prod/2002pubs/p23-210. pdf

Delpierre, C., Lauwers-Cances, V., Datta, G. D., Berkman, L., & Lang, T. (2009). Impact of social position on the effect of cardiovascular risk factors on self-rated health. *American Journal Of Public Health, 99*(7), 1278-1284.

Dewey J. (1916). *Democracy and education.* New York: The Free Press.

Dewey, J. (1938). *Experience and education.* New York: Kappa Delta Pi.

Dillman, D. A., Smyth, J. D., & Christian, L. M. (2009). *Internet, mail, and mixed-mode surveys: The tailored design method* (3rd ed.). Hoboken, NJ: John Wiley & Sons Inc.

Dodge, B. (1996). Distance learning on the World Wide Web: Computer training's personal trainer's guide. Retrieved on July 30, 2008, from http://edweb. sdsu. edu/People/Bdodge/ctptg/ctptg. html

Dueber, B. & Misanchuk, M. (2001). Sense of community in a distance education course. Paper presented at the Mid South Instructional Technology Conference, 8-10 April, Murfreesboro, TN. Retrieved from http://bill. dueber. com/dueber-misanchuk. pdf

Dwyer, D., Barbieri, K., & Doerr, H. (1995). Creating a virtual classroom for interactive education on the web. *Computer Networks and ISDN Systems, 27,* 897-904. Retrieved from Science Direct database.

Dziuban, C. & Moskal, P. (2001). Evaluating distributed learning at metropolitan universities. *Educause Quarterly, 24*(4), 60-61. Retrieved from http://net. educause. edu/ir/library/pdf/EQM01412. pdf

Dziuban, C., Hartman, J., & Moskal, P. (2004). Blended learning. *EDUCAUSE Center for Applied Research, Research Bulletin, 7.*

Emeagwali, N. (2007). Community colleges offer baby boomers an encore. *Techniques: Connecting Education & Careers, 82*(7), 18-19.

Epp, E. M., Green, K. F., Rahman, A. M., & Weaver, G. C. (2010). Analysis of student–instructor interaction patterns in real-time, scientific online discourse. *Journal Of Science Education & Technology, 19*(1), 49-57. doi:10.1007/s10956-009-9177-z

Falowo, R. O. (2007). Factors impeding implementation of web-based distance learning. *AACE Journal, 15*(3), 315-338. Retrieved on August 10, 2008, from EBSCO database.

File, T., & Crissey, S. R. (2010). *Voting and registration in the election of November 2008.* Current Population Reports. Washington : U. S. Census Bureau. Retrieved from http://www. census. gov/prod/2010pubs/p20-562. pdf

Gatto, S. L., & Tak, S. H. (2008). computer, Internet, and e-mail use among older adults: Benefits and barriers. *Educational Gerontology, 34*(9), 800-811. doi:10.1080/03601270802243697

George, D., & Mallery, P. (2011). *SPSS for windows step by step: A simple guide and reference 18. 0 update.* (11th ed.). Boston, MA: Allyn & Bacon.

Graf, M. (2003). Individual differences in sense of community in a blended learning environment. *Journal of Educational Media, 28*(2-3), 203-210. doi: 10. 1080/1358165032000165635

Haythornthwaite, C., Kazmer, M., Robins, J., & Shoemaker, S. (2000). Community development among distance learners: Temporal and technological dimensions. *Journal of Computer-Mediated Communication,* 6(1). Retrieved from http://jcmc. indiana. edu/vol6/issue1/haythornthwaite. html

Hemby, K. V. (1998). Self-directedness in non-traditional college students: A behavioral factor in computer anxiety? *Computers in Human Behavior, 14*(2), 303-319. Retrieved from Science Direct database.

Herring, M. C. (2004). Development of constructivist-based distance learning environments: A knowledge base for K-12 teachers. *The Quarterly Review of Distance Education, 5*(4), 231-242. Retrieved on August 1, 2008, from EBSCO database.

Hill, K., Hoffman, D., & Rex, T. R. (2005). The value of higher education: Individual and societal benefits (With special consideration for the State of Arizona). Retrieved from http://wpcarey. asu. edu/seid/upload/Value%20Full%20Report_final_october%202005a. pdf

Hoonakker, P., & Carayon, P. (2009). Questionnaire Survey Nonresponse: A Comparison of Postal Mail and Internet Surveys. *International Journal Of Human-Computer Interaction, 25*(5), 348-373. doi:10.1080/10447310902864951

Howell, D. C. (2004). *Fundamental statistics for the behavioral sciences* (5th ed.). Belmont, CA: Brooks/Cole.

Hrastinski, S. (2008). Asynchronous and synchronous e-learning. *EDUCAUSE*

Quarterly, 34(4). Retrieved from
http://www.educause.edu/EDUCAUSE+Quarterly/EDUCAUSEQuarterlyMa
gazineVolum/AsynchronousandSynchronousELea/163445

Huang, H. M. (2002). Toward constructivism for adult learners in online learning
environments. *British Journal of Educational Technology, 33*(1), 27-37.
Retrieved on August 5, 2008, from EBSCO database.

Hughes, M., & Daykin, N. (2002). Towards Constructivism: Investigating
Students' Perceptions and Learning as a Result of Using an Online
Environment. *Innovations in Education & Teaching International, 39*(3),
217-224. doi:10. 1080/13558000210150036

Irizarry, R. (2002). Self-efficacy and motivation effects on online psychology
student retention. *USDLA Journal, 16*(12), 55-64. Retrieved from
file:///M:/Irizarry%202002. html

Jonassen, D. H., Peck, K. L., & Wilson, B. G. (1999). *Learning with technology:
A constructivist perspective.* Upper Saddle River, NJ: Prentice Hall, Inc.

Jorgensen, D. (2002). The challenges and benefits of asynchronous learning
networks. *Distance Learning: Information and Services for Virtual Users*, 3-
17. Retrieved on August 2, 2008, from EBSCO database.

Jung, I., Choi, S., Lim, C., & Leem, J. (2002). Effects of different types of
interaction on learning achievement, satisfaction and participation in web-
based instruction. *Innovations in Education and Teaching International,
39*(2), 153-162. doi: 10. 1080/1355800021012139 9

Kala S., Isaramalai, S., & Pohthong, A. (2010). Electronic learning and
constructivism: A model for nursing education. *Nurse Education Today,
30*(1), 61-66. doi:10. 1016/j. nedt. 2009. 06. 002

Kassop, M. (2003). Ten ways online education matches, or surpasses, face-
to-face learning. Retrieved from http://technologysource.
org/article/ten_ways_online_education_matches_or_surpasses_facetofac
e_learning/?keepThis=true&TB_iframe=true&height=400&width=800

Kasworm, C. (2003). Adult meaning making in the undergraduate classroom.
Adult Education Quarterly. 53(2), 81-98.

Kawachi, P. (2003). Initiating intrinsic motivation in online education: Review of
the current state of art. *Interactive Learning Environments, 11*(1), 59-91.
doi:1049-4820/03/1101-59

Kilpatrick, L. A., & Feeney, B. C. (2007). *SPSS for windows step by step: A
simple guide and reference 15.0 update (8th ed.).* Pearson Education, Inc.

Kinney, N. E. (2001). A guide to design and testing in online psychology
courses. *Psychology Learning and Teaching, 1*(1), 16-20. Retrieved on
July 15, 2008, from http://www. psychology. heacademy. ac.
uk/docs/pdf/p20021021_kinney0. pdf

Kozlowski, D. (2002). Returning to school: An alternative to 'traditional'
education. *Orthopaedic Nursing, 21*(4), 41-47. Retrieved on August 1,
2008, from EBSCO database.

Lee, J., Carter-Wells, J., Gleser, B., Ivers, K., & Street, C. (2006). Facilitating
the development of a learning community in an online graduate program.
The Quarterly Review of Distance Education, 7(1):13-33. Retrieved from
EBSCO database.

Lee, Z., & Woodliffe, L. (2010). Donor Misreporting: Conceptualizing Social
Desirability Bias in Giving Surveys. *Voluntas: International Journal Of
Voluntary & Nonprofit Organizations, 21*(4), 569-587. doi:10.1007/s11266-
010-9153-5

Lefoe, G. (1998). Creating constructivist learning environments on the Web: The challenge in higher education. Centre for Educational Development and Interactive Resources, University of Wollongong, Australia. Retrieved on July 15, 2008, from http://www. ascilite. org. au/conferences/wollongong98/asc98-pdf/lefoe00162. pdf

Leist, J., & Travis, J. (2010). Planning for online courses at rural community colleges. *New Directions For Community Colleges*, (150), 17-25. doi:10.1002/cc.401

Levin, H., Belfield, C., Muennig, P., & Rouse, C. (2007). The costs and benefits of an excellent education of all of America's children. Retrieved from https://www. ofy. org/uploaded/library/Leeds_Report_Final_Jan2007. pdf

Lino, M. (2011). Expenditures on Children by Families, 2010. U. S. Department of Agriculture, Center for Nutrition Policy and Promotion. Miscellaneous Publication No. 1528-2010. Retrieved from http://www. cnpp. usda. gov/Publications/CRC/crc2010. pdf

Lipsey, M., & Wilson, D. (1993). The efficacy of psychological, educational, and behavioral treatment: Confirmation from meta-analysis. *American Psychologist, 48*(12), 1181-1209. doi: 10.1037/0003-066X.48.12.1181

Liu, X., Magjuka, R. J., Bonk, C. J., & Seung-Jee, L. (2007). Does sense of community matter? An examination of participants' perceptions of building learning communities in online courses. *Quarterly Review of Distance Education, 8*(1), 9-24.

Lokken, F., & Womer, L. (2007). Trends in e-learning: Tracking the impact of e-learning in higher education. 2006 Distance education survey results. Washington, DC: Instructional Technology Council. Retrieved on August 5, 2008 from http://www. itcnetwork. org/file. php?file=/1/ITCAnnualSurveyFeb2007. pdf.

Lord, G., & Lomicka, L. (2008). Blended learning in teacher education: An investigation of classroom community across media. *Contemporary Issues in Technology and Teacher Education, 8*(2). Retrieved from http://www. citejournal. org/vol8/iss2/general/article1. cfm

McGorry, S. Y. (2002). Measuring quality in online education. Internet and Higher Education, 6, 159-177. doi:10. 1016/S1096-7516(03)00022-8

McInnerney, J. M., & Roberts, T. S. (2004). Online Learning: Social Interaction and the Creation of a Sense of Community. *Educational Technology & Society, 7*(3), 73-81.

Merriam, S. B., & Caffarella, R. S. (1999). *Learning in adulthood: A comprehensive guide. (2nd ed.).* San Francisco: Jossey-Bass Inc., Publishers.

Mertler, C. A., & Vanatta, R. A. (2005). *Advanced and multivariate statistical methods (3rd ed.)* Glendale, CA; Pyrzcak Publishing.

Michael Blocher, J. J. (2005). Increasing learner interaction: using Jigsaw online. *Educational Media International, 42*(3), 269-278. doi:10. 1080/09523980500161486

Miller, M. T., & Lu, M. Y. (2002). Barriers and challenges to serving non-traditional students in e-learning environments. Retrieved from ERIC database. (ED468117)

Miller, M. T., & Mei-Yan, L. (2003). Serving non-traditional students in e-learning environments: Building successful communities in the virtual campus. *Educational Media International, 40*(1/2), 163.

Mirakian, E. A., & Hale, L. S. (2007). A comparison of online instruction vs.

traditional classroom instruction in an undergraduate pharmacology course. Proceeding of the 3rd Annual GRASP Symposium, Wichita State University. Retrieved from http://soar. wichita. edu/dspace/bitstream/handle/10057/721/96. pdf;jsessionid=45C508521735BD796BD0A16EA5BD3A3B?sequence=1

Misanchuk, M., & Anderson, T. (2001, April). *Building community in an online learning environment: Communication, cooperation, and collaboration.* Paper presented at the Mid-South Instructional Technology Conference, Murfreesboro, TN. Retrieved from http://www.mtsu.edu/~itconf/proceed01/19.html

Monroe, A. (2006). Non-traditional transfer student attrition. Community College Enterprise, *12*(2), 33-54. Retrieved from http://www. schoolcraft. edu/pdfs/cce/12. 2. 33-54. pdf

Mortagy, Y., & Boghikian-Whitby, S. (2010). A Longitudinal Comparative Study of Student Perceptions in Online Education. *Interdisciplinary Journal of E-Learning & Learning Objects*, 623-44. Retrieved from EBSCO*host*.

Moskal, P. D., & Dziuban, C. D. (2001). Present and future directions for assessing cybereducation: The changing research paradigm. In L. R. Vandervert, L. V. Shavinina, & R. A. Cornell (Eds.), *Cybereducation: The future of long-distance learning* (pp. 157–184). New York: Mary Ann Liebert.

Moskal, P., Dziuban, C., Upchurch, R., Hartman, J., & Truman, B. (2006). Assessing Online Learning: What One University Learned about Student Success, Persistence, and Satisfaction. *Peer Review, 8*(4), 26-29. Retrieved from EBSCO*host*.

Moutray, C. (2009). Educational attainment, "brain drain," and self employment: Examining the interstate mobility of baccalaureate graduates, 1993 - 2003. U. S. Small Business Administration , Office of Advocacy. Retrieved from http://www. sba. gov/sites/default/files/Educational%20Attainment. pdf

National Association of Child Care Resource & Referral Agencies. (2011). Child care in America: 2011 state facts sheets. Retrieved from http://www.naccrra.org/publications/naccrra-publications/publications/ChildCareInAmericaFacts%20Full%20Report-2011.pdf

National Association of Child Care Resource & Referral Agencies. (2011). Child care in America: 2011 state facts sheets. Retrieved from http://www.naccrra.org/publications/naccrra-publications/publications/ChildCareInAmericaFacts%20Full%20Report-2011.pdf

National Center for Education Statistics. (2009). Digest for education

National Center for Educational Statistics. (1999). Distance education at postsecondary education institutions: 1997 - 98. Retrieved from http://nces. ed. gov/surveys/peqis/publications/2000013/index. asp?sectionID=8

National Center for Educational Statistics. (2003). Distance education at degree-granting postsecondary institutions: 2000-2001. Executive summary. Retrieved on August 1, 2008, from http://nces. ed. gov/surveys/peqis/publications/2003017/

National Center for Educational Statistics. (2011). Fast facts. Retrieved from http://nces. ed. gov/fastfacts/display. asp?id=27

Northern Maine Community College. (n.d.). About NMCC. Retrieved from http://www.nmcc.edu/pages/nmcc/about-nmcc.php

Norusis, M. (2006). *SPSS 15.0: Guide to data analysis*. Upper Saddle River, NJ: Prentice Hall.

O'Lawrence, H. (2007). An overview of the influences of distance learning on adult learners. *Journal of Education and Human Development* [On-line], 1(1). Retrieved on August 5, 2008, from http://www. scientificjournals. org/journals2007/articles/1041. htm

Ornstein, A. C., & Hunkins, F. P. (2009). Curriculum: Foundations, principles, and issues (5th ed.). Boston, MA: Allyn & Bacon.

Ouzts, K. (2006). Sense of community in online courses. *Quarterly Review of Distance Education, 7*(3), 285-296, 346. Retrieved on September 10, 2009, from ProQuest database.

Overbaugh, R. C., & Nickel, C. E. (2010). A comparison of student satisfaction and value of academic community between blended and online sections of a university-level educational foundations course, *The Internet and Higher Education*. doi: 10. 1016/j. iheduc. 2010. 12. 001

Palmer, S. R., & Holt, D. M. (2009). Examining student satisfaction with wholly online learning. *Journal of Computer Assisted Learning, 25*(2), 101-113. doi:10. 1111/j. 1365-2729. 2008. 00294. x

Parloff, R. M., & Pratt, K. (2007). Building online learning communities: Effective strategies for the virtual classroom. San Francisco, CA: John Wiley & Sons.

Parsad, B., & Lewis, L. (2008). *Distance education at degree-granting postsecondary institutions: 2006–07* (NCES 2009–044). National Center for Education Statistics, Institute of Education Sciences, U. S. Department of Education. Washington, DC. Retrieved February 18, 2010, from http://nces. ed. gov/pubsearch/pubsinfo. asp?pubid=2009044

Patsula, P. J. (1999). Applying learning theories to online instructional design. Retrieved on July 13, 2008, from http://www. patsula. com/usefo/webbasedlearning/tutorial1/learning_theories_full_version. html

Phinney, J. S., Dennis, J., & Osorio, S. (2006). Reasons to attend college among ethnically diverse college students. *Cultural Diversity and Ethnic Minority Psychology, 12*(2), 347-366. doi:10. 1037/1099-9809. 12. 2. 347

Piaget J (1973). *To understand is to invent: The future of education* New York: Grossman.

Pigliapoco, E., & Bogliolo A. (2007). The effects of the psychological sense of community in on-line and face-to-face academic courses, *Conference on Interactive Computer Aided Learning*, September 26 -28, 2007, Villach, Austria. Retrieved from http://telearn. archives-ouvertes. fr/docs/00/19/72/37/PDF/71_Final_Paper. pdf

Qureshi, E., Morton, L. L., & Antonsz, E. (2002). An interesting profile-university students who take distance education courses sow weaker motivation than on-campus students. *Online Journal of Distance Education Learning Administration, 5*(4). Retrieved from http://distance. westga. edu/~distance/ojdla/winter54/Quershi54. htm

Richmond, V. P., Gorham, J. S., & McCroskey, J. C. (1987). The relationship between selected immediacy behaviors and cognitive learning. In M. A. McLaughlin (Ed.), Communication yearbook, vol. 10 (pp. 574–590). Newbury Park, CA: Sage.

Ritter, C., Polnick, B., Fink, , R., & Oescher, J. (2010). Classroom learning communities in educational leadership: A comparison study of three delivery options. *Internet and Higher Education*, 13, 96–100.

doi:10.1016/j.iheduc.2009.11.005

Rose, S. (2010). Connectivity: A Framework for Understanding Effective Language Teaching in Face-to-face and Online Learning Communities. *RELC Journal, 41*(2), 137-147. doi:10. 1177/0033688210375775

Rovai, A. P. (2001). Building classroom community at a distance: A case study. *Education Technology and Research Development, 49*(4), 33-48.

Rovai, A. P. (2002a). Development of an instrument to measure classroom community. *The Internet and Higher Education, 5*, 197-211.

Rovai, A. P. (2002b). A Preliminary look at the structural differences of higher education: Classroom communities in traditional and ALN courses. *Journal of Asynchronous Learning Networks, 6*(1), 41-56.

Rovai, A. P. (2002c). Sense of community, perceived cognitive learning, and persistence in asynchronous learning networks. *The Internet and Higher Education, 5*(4), 319-332.

Rovai, A. P. (2007). Facilitating online discussions effectively. *Internet and Higher Education, 10*, 77-88. doi: 10. 1016. j. iheduc. 2006. 10. 001

Rovai, A. P., & Baker, J. D. (2005). Gender differences in online learning: Sense of community, perceived learning, and interpersonal interactions. *Quarterly Review of Distance Education, 6*(1), 31-44.

Rovai, A. P., & Barnum, K. T. (2003). On-line course effectiveness: An analysis of student interactions and perceptions of learning. *Journal of Distance Education, 18*(1), 57-73.

Rovai, A. P., & Jordan, H. M. (2004). Blended learning and sense of community: A comparative analysis with traditional and fully online graduate courses. *The International Review of Research in Open and Distance Learning, 5*(2). Retrieved from http://www. irrodl. org/index. php/irrodl/article/view/192/274

Rovai, A. P., & Lucking, R. (2003). Sense of Community in a Higher Education Television-Based Distance Education Program. *Educational Technology Research and Development, 51*(2), 5-16. Retrieved on July 30, 2009, from PsycARTICLES database.

Rovai, A. P., & Lucking, R. A. (2000, September). *Measuring sense of classroom community.* Paper presented at Learning 2000: Reassessing the Virtual University, Virginia Tech, Roanoke, VA.

Rovai, A. P., & Ponton, M. K. (2205). An examination of sense of classroom community and learning among African American and Caucasian graduate students. *Journal of Asynchronous Learning Networks, 9*, 77-92.

Rovai, A. P., & Wighting, M. J. (2005). Feelings of alienation and community among higher education students in a virtual classroom. *Internet and Higher Education, 8*(2), 97–110.

Rovai, A. P., Wighting, M. J., & Jing, L. (2005). School climate. *Quarterly Review Of Distance Education, 6*(4), 361-374.

Rovai, A., Cristol, D. S., & Lucking, R. (2001). *Building classroom community at a distance.* Paper presented at American Educational Research Association Annual Meeting, Seattle, WA, April 12, 2001.

Ryan R. M., & Deci E. L. (2000) Self-determination theory and the facilitation of intrinsic motivation, social development, and well being. *American Psychologist 55*, 68–78. doi:10. 1006/ceps. 1999. 1020

Saad, L. (2002). Tobacco and smoking. *Gallup Poll Special Reports.* Retrieved from http://www. gallup. com/poll/9910/tobacco-smoking. aspx

Schweir, R., & Balbar, D. (2002). The interplay of content and community in synchronous and asynchronous communications: Virtual communication in a graduate seminar. *Canadian Journal of Learning and Technology, 28*(2), 21-30.

Shea, P. J. (2006). A study of students' sense of learning community in online learning environments. *Journal of Asynchronous Learning Networks, 10*(1). Retrieved March, 26, 2009, from http://www. sloanc. org/publications/jaln/v10n1/v10n1_4shea_member. asp

Shea, P., Li, C. S., & Pickett, A., (2006). A study of teaching presence and student sense of learning community in fully online and web-enhanced college courses. *Internet and Higher Education, 9*, 175-190. DOI: 10. 1016/j. iheduc. 2006. 06. 005

Shen, D., Nuankhieo, P., Huang, X., Amelung, C., & Laffey, J. (2008). Using social network analysis to understand sense of community in an online learning environment. *Journal of Educational Computing Research, 39*(1), 17-36. Retrieved on July 30, 2009, from PsycARTICLES database.

Sherry, L. (1996). Issues in distance learning. *International Journal of Educational Telecommunications, 1*(4), 337-365.

Steele, M. M. (2005). Teaching students with learning disabilities: *Constructivism or behaviorism? Current Issues in Education* [On-line], *8*(10). Retrieved on June 21, 2008, from http://cie. asu. edu/volume8/number10/

Stephens, J. P. (2009). *Applied multivariate statistics for the social sciences (*5th *ed.).* New York, NY: Routledge.

Stepich, D. A., & Ertmer, P. A. (2003). Building community as a critical element of online course design. *Educational Technology, 43*(5), 33-43.

Stevens, T., & Switzer, C. (2006). Differences between online and traditional students: A study motivational orientation, self-efficacy, and attitudes. *Turkish Online Journal of Distance Education, 7*(2), 90-100. ED494394

Sthapornnanon, N., Sakulbumrungsil, R., Theeraroungchaisri, A., & Watcharadamrongkun, S. (2009). Social Constructivist Learning Environment in an Online Professional Practice Course. *American Journal of Pharmaceutical Education, 73*(1), 1-8. Retrieved from EBSCO*host*.

Stodel E. J., Thompson, T. L., & MacDonald, C. J. (2006). Learners' Perspectives on What is Missing from Online Learning: Interpretations through the Community of Inquiry Framework. *The International Review of Research in Open and Distance Learning, 7*. Retrieved January 5, 2011, from http://www. irrodl. org/index. php/irrodl/article/viewArticle/325/743

Stoops, N. (2004). *Educational attainment in the United States 2003.* Current Population Reports. Washington : U. S. Census Bureau. Retrieved from http://www. census. gov/prod/2004pubs/p20-550. pdf

Stover, C. (2005). Measuring--and Understanding--Student Retention. *Distance Education Report, 9*(16), 1-7.

Swan, K. (2001). Virtual interaction: Design factors affecting student satisfaction and perceived learning in asynchronous online courses. *Distance Education, 22*(2), 306-331. doi: 10. 1080/0158791010220208

Swan, K. (2002). Building learning communities in online courses: The importance of interaction. *Education, Communication & Information, 2*(1):23-49. doi: 10. 1080/1463631022000000501-6

Swan, K. (2003). Learning effectiveness online: What the research tells us. In J. Bourne & J. C. Moore (Eds). *Elements of Quality Online Education, Practice and Direction.* Needham, MA: Sloan Center for Online Education,

13-45.

Swan, K., Shea, P., Fredericksen, E., Pickett, A., Pelz, W., & Maher, G. (2000). Building knowledge building communities: Consistency, contact and communication in the virtual classroom, *Journal of Educational Computing Research, 23,* 389–413.

Taniguchi, H., & Kaufman, G. (2007). Belated entry: Gender differences and similarities in the pattern of non-traditional college enrollment. *Social Science Research, 36,* 550-568. doi: 10.016/j.ssresearch.2006.03.003

Tanner, L. (2007). *Critical challenges and barriers to online learning- Non-traditional adult students in a non-traditional teacher licensing program.* Saarbrücken, Germany: VDM Verlag.

Terry, N. (2001). N. (2001). Assessing enrollment and attrition rates for the online MBA. *T H E Journal, 28*(7), 64-68. Retrieved from http://thejournal. com/articles/2001/02/01/assessing-enrollment-and-attrition-rates-for-the-online-mba. aspx

Thomas, K. Q. (2001). Local colleges providing online learning programs. *Rochester Business Journal, 16*(43). Retrieved from http://www. rbj. net/article. asp?aID=126929

Tinto, V. (1994). *Leaving college: Rethinking the causes and cures of student attrition.* Chicago, IL: University of College Press.

Tinto, V. (1997). Classrooms as communities. *Journal of Higher Education, 68*(6), 599–623. Retrieved June 16, 2011, from Research Library. (Document ID: 22494915).

Tu, C.-H., & Corry. M. (2001). A paradigm shift for online community research. *Distance Education, 22*(2), 245-263.

U. S. Department of Education National Center for Education Statistics (1999). *Distance education at postsecondary education institutions: 1997-98.* NCES 2000-013, by Laurie Lewis, Kyle Snow, Elizabeth Farris, Douglas Levin. Bernie Greene, project officer. Washington, DC: Author. Retrieved January 3, 2004 from http://nces. ed. gov/pubs2000/2000013. pdf

U. S. Department of Education. (2009). *Evaluation of evidence-based practices in online learning: A meta-analysis and review of online learning studies.* Washington, DC: Office of Planning, Evaluation, and Policy Development.

U. S. Department of Health and Human Services. (2009). Code of federal regulations. Retrieved from http://www.hhs.gov/ohrp/humansubjects/guidance/45cfr46. html

U.S. Department of Education, National Center for Education Statistics. (2011). *Digest of Education Statistics, 2010* (NCES 2011-015),

U.S. Department of Education. National Center for Education Statistics. (2002). Profile of undergraduates in U.S. postsecondary education institutions: 1999–2000. NCES Publication No. 2002–168.

Vygotsky, L. S. (1978). *Mind in society: The development of higher psychological processes.* MA: Harvard University Press.

Waits, T., & Lewis, L. (2003). *Distance education at degree-granting postsecondary institutions: 2000-2001* (NCES 2003-017). Washington, DC: US Department of Education, National Center for Education Statistics. Retrieved on August 10, 208, from http://nces. ed. gov/pubs2003/2003017. pdf

Washington County Community College. (2010). Accreditation. Retrieved from http://www. wccc. me. edu/index. php?option=com_content&view=category&layout=blog&id=26&Itemid=52

Weasenforth, D., Biesenback-Lucas, S., & Meloni, C. (2002, September). Realizing constructivist objectives through collaborative technologies: Threaded discussions. *Language Learning and Technology, 6*(3), 58-86.

Webb Boyd, P. (2008). Analyzing Students' Perceptions of Their Learning in Online and Hybrid First-Year Composition Courses. *Computers and Composition, 25*, 224-243. DOI: 10. 1016/j. compcom. 2008. 01. 002

WebCT campus edition™ 4. 1 release notes. (2003). Retrieved from http://www. polyu. edu. hk/webbt/41_CE_releasenote. html

Wegerif, R. (1998). The social dimension of asynchronous learning networks. *Journal of Asynchronous Learning Networks, 2* [Online]. Retrieved from http://citeseerx.ist. psu. edu/viewdoc/download?doi=10. 1. 1. 103. 7298&rep=rep1&type=pdf

Wighting, M. J, Liu, J., & Rovai, A. P. (2008). Distinguishing sense of community and motivation characteristics between online and traditional college students. *Quarterly Review of Distance Education, 9*(3), 285-295. Retrieved on January 30, 2010, from EBSCO database.

Wilson, B., & Lowry, M. (2000). *Constructivist learning on the Web.* Retrieved on July 16, 2008, from http://carbon. cudenver. edu/~bwilson/WebLearning. html

Wlodkowski, R. J., Mauldin, J., & Campbell, S. (2002). Early exit: Understanding adult attrition in accelerated and traditional postsecondary programs. Synopsis: Higher Education Research Highlights. Retrieved from http://www. luminafoundation. org/publications/synopsis/Earlyexit02. pdf

Woo, Y., & Reeves, T. C. (2007). Meaningful interaction in web-based learning: A social constructivist interpretation. *Internet & Higher Education, 10*(1), 15-25. doi:10. 1016/j. iheduc. 2006. 10. 005

Xu, D., & Smith Jaggers, S. (2011). Online and hybrid course enrollment and performance in Washington State community and technical colleges. Community College Research Center, Working Paper No. 31. Retrieved from http://ccrc. tc. columbia. edu/Publication. asp?UID=872

Young, S., & Bruce, M. A. (2011). Classroom community and student engagement in online courses. *Journal of Online Learning and Teaching, 7*(2). Retrieved from http://jolt. merlot. org/vol7no2/young_0611. htm

APPENDICES

Appendix A: Letter of Cooperation

Washington County Community College
One College rive
Calais, Maine, 04619

December 22,2011

Institutional Review Board
Walden University
155 5th Avenue Minneapolis, MN 55401

To Whom It May Concern:

Patricia Giero has requested permission to collect research data from students at Washington County Community College. I have been informed of the purposes of the study and the nature of the research procedures. I have also been given an opportunity to ask questions of the researcher.

As a representative of Washington County Community College, I am authorized to grant permission to have the researcher recruit research participants from our school.

If you have any questions, please contact me at, XXX

Sincerely,
(signature) David Markow
Dean of Academic and Student Affairs Washington County Community College One College Drive
Calais, Maine 04619

Appendix B: Participant Invitation Letter

Dear Washington Community College Students,

My name is Patsy Giero, and I am a graduate student in the School of Psychology at Walden University. With increasing numbers of students both traditional and non-traditional seeking a college degree, many enroll in online, hybrid, or online courses to attend college courses. This may pose many challenges for both work and family.

The purpose of this study is to investigate sense of community among traditional and non-traditional students enrolled in online, hybrid, and traditional land-based learning environments at a rural community college. Would you be willing to assist me in some very exciting research that explores the relationship between sense of community (defined as a feeling of connectedness and sense of belonging members share along with group norms and values and the extent to which their educational goals and expectations are satisfied by group membership) and the different types of learning environments?

I am looking for any student who is currently enrolled in a degree program. If you fit this criteria, I would greatly appreciate your participation in this study.

I realize your obligations to your career and to your family not to mention to your classes. All these obligations provide little time to participate in research projects. However, successful research in this area will ultimately benefit the student. Your participation would take less than thirty minutes of your time and involve completing a confidential and anonymous online survey designed to measure your sense of community.

Below you will find the website at which you can complete the online survey. You can either click on the link or cut and paste the address into your web browser's address bar.

Please be aware that because your participation is anonymous, you must complete the survey in one sitting. There is no way to link your responses to your identity if you attempt to log in again at a later time.

If you have any questions related to this research, I would be happy to answer them. Feel free to contact me using the information listed below. Thank you for considering being a part of this most exciting adventure.

Sincerely,

Patsy Giero, M.S.
Graduate Student in General Psychology
School of Psychology, Walden University

Website: https://www.surveymonkey.com/s/FMLFTMT

Appendix C: Letter of Permission of CCS

Original E-mail

From: Alfred Rovai
Date: 02/13/2011 12:49 PM
To: Patricia Giero
Subject: RE: Request Permission

Hi Patricia,

Yes, you may use the instrument for your dissertation research.

The only requirement is that you cite the source article in any report you write: Rovai, A. P. (2002). Development of an instrument to measure classroom community.

Internet & Higher Education, 5(3), 197-211. (ERIC Document Reproduction Service No. EJ663068)

Best wishes,

Fred

Alfred P. Rovai, Ph. D.
Interim VP for Academic Affairs, Regent University
1000 Regent University Drive, Virginia Beach, VA 23464

Appendix D: Informed Consent Form

You are invited to take part in a research study of Sense of Community and Online Learning. You were chosen for the study because you are currently enrolled at Washington County Community College (WCCC) or Northern Maine Community College (NMCC). This form is part of a process called "informed consent" and the purpose of the form is to explain this study before deciding whether to take part.

This study is being conducted by a researcher named Patricia Giero, who is a doctoral student at Walden University.

Background Information:

The purpose of this study is to examine student perceptions of sense of community in online courses. Specifically, The purpose of this is to investigate sense of community among traditional and non-traditional students enrolled in online, hybrid, and traditional land-based learning environments at a rural community college.

Procedures:

If you agree to be in this study, you will be asked to complete the survey. The survey will take approximately *30 minutes* to complete.

Voluntary Nature of the Study:

Your participation in this study is voluntary. This means that everyone will respect your decision of whether or not you want to be in the study. No one at WCCC or NMCC will treat you differently if you decide not to be in the study. If you decide to join the study now, you can still change your mind during the study. If you feel stressed during the study you may stop at any time.

Risks and Benefits of Being in the Study:

The risks associated with this study are minimal. The only foreseeable risk is boredom from taking the survey. However, the benefits do make it worthwhile for this educational institution.

The benefit of being in this study provides valuable information that will potentially assist rural community colleges in expanding their online courses and programs in order to meet the growing needs of the community and to catch up on the growing trends of online education. I cannot and do not guarantee or promise that you will receive any benefits from this study.

Compensation:

Compensation will not be provided for participating in the study.

Confidentiality:

Any information you provide will be kept <u>confidential</u>. The researcher will not use your information for any purposes outside of this research project. Also, the researcher will not include your name or anything else that could identify you in any reports of the study. The website used for this study uses industry standard SSL encryption to ensure the secure transmission of the data you enter. If you are not comfortable in participating in this online study, you may click "I Disagree" to exit the survey. You are encouraged to keep/print a copy of the consent form for your records. Click on the button on the screen labeled "Print" to print a copy of the form for you records.

Upon completion of this study, the findings and results will be shared with Washington County Community College, if you would like a copy for your records. A copy may be found in the library and on the shared drive of WCCC. An e-mailed copy will be forwarded to the Dean of Academics, David Markow. Also, the findings and results will be shared with Northern Maine Community College, if you would like a copy for your records. An e-mailed copy will be forwarded to the President, Timothy Crowley.

Contacts and Questions:

You may ask any questions you have now. Or if you have questions later, you may contact the researcher via email at, patricia.giero@waldenu.edu or at, 207.726.9573. If you want to talk privately about your rights as a participant, you can call Dr. Leilani Endicott. She is the Walden University representative who can discuss this with you. Her phone number is 1-800-925-3368, extension 1210. Walden University's approval number for this study is 02-01-12-0114628 and it expires on January 31, 2013.

Statement of Consent:

Please read the following statement and click "I Agree" below to indicate that you understand and agree to the terms outline by this consent form and with to proceed as a participant If you do not wish to participate in the study, click on "I Disagree."

"I have read the above explanation of this study and I agree to participate. I understand that my responses will be anonymous and will be kept confidential. I understand my participation in this study is voluntary and I may discontinue my participation at any time without penalty."

Appendix E: Sense of Community Survey

Below, you will see a series of statements concerning a specific course or program you are presently taking. Read each statement carefully and CLICK on the response that comes closest to indicate how you feel about the course or program. There are no correct or incorrect responses. If you neither agree nor disagree with a statement or are uncertain, CLICK on the Neutral response. Do not spend too much time on any one statement, but give the best response that seems to describe how you feel.

Please respond to all items.

1. I feel students in this course care about each other.
    Strongly   Agree   Neutral   Disagree   Strongly

2. I feel I am encouraged to ask questions.
    Strongly   Agree   Neutral   Disagree   Strongly

3. I feel connected to others in this course.
    Strongly   Agree   Neutral   Disagree   Strongly

4. I feel It is hard to get help when I have a question.
    Strongly   Agree   Neutral   Disagree   Strongly

5. I do not feel a spirit of community.
    Strongly   Agree   Neutral   Disagree   Strongly

6. I feel I receive timely feedback.
   Strongly   Agree   Neutral   Disagree   Strongly

7. I feel this course is like a family,
   Strongly   Agree   Neutral   Disagree   Strongly

8. I feel uneasy exposing gaps in my understanding.
   Strongly   Agree   Neutral   Disagree   Strongly

9. I feel isolated in this course.
   Strongly   Agree   Neutral   Disagree   Strongly

10. I feel reluctant to speak openly.
    Strongly   Agree   Neutral   Disagree   Strongly

11. I trust others in this course.
    Strongly   Agree   Neutral   Disagree   Strongly
12. I feel this course results in only modest learning.
    Strongly   Agree   Neutral   Disagree   Strongly

13. I feel I can rely on others in this course.
    Strongly   Agree   Neutral   Disagree   Strongly

14. I feel other students do not help me learn.
    Strongly   Agree   Neutral   Disagree   Strongly

15. I feel members of this course depend on me.
    Strongly   Agree   Neutral   Disagree   Strongly

16. I feel I am given ample opportunities to learn.
    Strongly   Agree   Neutral   Disagree   Strongly

17. I feel uncertain about others in this course.
    Strongly   Agree   Neutral   Disagree   Strongly

18. I feel that my educational needs are not being met.
    Strongly   Agree   Neutral   Disagree   Strongly

19. I feel confident others will support me.
    Strongly   Agree   Neutral   Disagree   Strongly

20.I feel this course does not promote a desire to learn.
    Strongly   Agree   Neutral   Disagree   Strongly

INDEX

CURRICULUM VITAE

Patricia A. Giero, Ph.D., LSW-C
Perry, Maine

TEACHING PHILOSPHY

My teaching philosophy reflects my interests and passion in learning. Education is a life-long endeavor and as educators, our goal is to prepare students for this endeavor by providing the students with a base of information on which they can build, and encouraging in them attitudes and techniques for continued learning. I prefer student-centered teaching that encourages learning by both students and teachers. I believe that teaching should be a creative and meaningful endeavor for both the teacher and the student. There should be constant communication between the teacher and learner so that any difficulties that arise may be resolved as soon as possible so the learning process may continue.

Students have different learning styles and cannot be expected to absorb material in the same way all of the time, so it is necessary to vary instructional methods to give students the chance to learn. I favor classroom dynamics that permit dialogue and foster a degree of student input as to curricula and grading criteria. Finally, I like students to think about the class as a learning community, which is evidenced by active participation from both the students and me in the learning community.

PERSONAL ATTRIBUTES

- Experienced in teaching and facilitating online, blended, and traditional courses in areas of psychology, sociology, ethics, introduction to philosophy, criminological theory with over eight years of experience in delivering Distance Education

- Experienced in development and writing of online psychology courses
- Experienced in coordinating and supervising student internships for the Criminal Justice program at WCCC
- Two years' experience in facilitating psycho-educational groups and counseling of convicted adult male sex offenders
- Experienced in managing and supervising instructors for the American Red Cross' Health & Safety program
- Proficient with eRacer, WebCT, BlackBoard, e-Campus, and eCollege online learning platforms

ACADEMIC EXPERIENCE

Summary:

- Adjunct faculty for Washington County Community College (WCCC).
- Adult literacy tutor training facilitator for Mayor's Commission on Literacy.
- Facilitates online courses for two online universities: the University of Phoenix and DeVry University.
- Advisor for the Criminal Justice program at WCCC.
- Coordinate and supervise student internships for the Criminal Justice program at WCCC.
- Development and writing of online psychology courses.
- Teaching online, blended, and traditional courses in areas of psychology, sociology, ethics, and introduction to philosophy, and criminological theory with over seven years of experience in delivering distance education.

TEACHING PORTFOLIO

10/15 to present
Adult Literacy Tutor Training Facilitator
Mayor's Commission on Literacy
Philadelphia, PA

- Provides volunteer tutors with strategies and resources to use when working with adult learners who are enrolled in

basic literacy programs, are preparing to pass the GED® exam and/or are working on improving their English language skills
- Facilitates online training sessions
- Facilitates and monitoring online training by monitoring trainees' enrollment in and completion of the online tutor training, including:
- Posting several encouraging announcements, at least once a week
- Reviewing and responding to the trainees' posts and submissions a minimum of four times week
- Stimulating discussions to maintain trainees' engagement
- Responding to trainees' online posts no more than 24 hours of their posting/submission
- Contacting trainees who are falling behind in the course electronically and/or by phone
- Submits training reports that summarize the number of attendees, activities undertaken during the online training, and provide recommendations

08/07 to present
Adjunct Faculty
Washington County Community College
Calais, ME

- PHI 101 – Introduction to Philosophy: This course is a study of the perennial problems of philosophy as discussed by authors of all periods, from the Pre-Socratic Greeks to contemporary writers. This survey focuses primarily on western philosophy, but also introduces eastern thought. Such issues as free will vs. determinism, the problem of evil, the mind-body split, the nature of time, the limits of science and mysticism are among topics offered.

- PHI 115 – Applied Ethics: This course provides the student with the knowledge of ancient and modern philosophies and ethical theories, provides opportunities to examine moral contemporary issues and to evaluate the actions that significantly harm and/or benefit humankind.

- PSY 101 – Introduction to Psychology: This course is an introduction in the discipline of psychology. The student will be able to define and describe the science of psychology and demonstrate knowledge of theoretical issues, psychological processes, and mechanisms of behavior.
- PSY 105 -- Human Relations: Human Relations introduces students to the principles of psychology applied to the understanding of self and others. Students will study the interactions that exist between people at work, in organizations and in one's personal life. The student will be provided with a clear, insightful, and comprehensive understanding to the principles and underlying psychological dynamics of interpersonal relations and have the opportunity to practice these skills.

- PSY 195 – Child & Adolescent Psychology: This course explores the growth and development of the child from conception through adolescence. Investigations of the physical, cognitive, and social-emotional domains are used to understand and describe the developing person. Students will understand the theories, research, and the multiple variables that affect the growth and development of children and adolescents. This is the second core course in the CDA certification series. The CDA certificate topics covered are: language and literacy development; literacy and the acquisition of second languages; development; cognition; discovery and problem solving; children as individuals; peer relationships and developing values; positive child guidance/discipline; observing and recording behavior; inclusion of children with disabilities; children at risk, developing self-esteem; developing identity, and the influence of family, peers, and community.

- PSY 207-Developmental Psychology: The development of the individual is an exciting process, beginning at birth and continuing through the intricate changes of growth and aging. The study of the life span is also intriguing because each of us, and everyone we care about, is constantly developing. This course therefore includes the biosocial, cognitive and psychosocial domains of human development.

- SOC 101 – Introduction to Sociology: This course is a general study of people in society, with emphasis on the nature of culture, social institutions, social interaction and social units and their influence on the individual. An overview of sociological concepts and perspectives is also presented.

- SOC 102 – Sociology of the Family: This course is an introduction to sociology, with an emphasis on family systems. Foundational sociological theory will be covered as a basis for an in-depth study of modern family structures. This course will explore the contemporary issues of power relationships; family organization and reorganization; single parent families; divorce, family violence, malfunction; and the effect of the family on the socialization of children.

- ENG 107 – Speech: This oral communication course offers experience in the selection and organization of speech content, audience analysis, and delivery. Classroom experience emphasizes preparation and delivery of informative and persuasive speeches, as well as other types of oral presentations.

- SED230 - Behavior Management Techniques: This course is designed to provide students with the knowledge and skills necessary to deal more effectively with students with emotional and behavioral difficulties. The emphasis of the course will be on the use of data collection to better understand how to intervene and change negative behaviors. Course content will emphasize both formal and informal data gathering techniques. Students will be taught how to select, plot, and interpret student self-control, self-esteem, and social skill problems. Crisis management techniques and the development of behavior management plans will be covered.

08/08 to present
Faculty
University of Phoenix
Phoenix, AZ

- PSY 201- Foundations of Psychology: This course overviews the foundations of psychology as the field applies to everyday life. The physical and mental aspects of psychology are traced through lifespan development with emphasis on psychological health and wellness. Further study focuses on personality; thinking, learning and memory; motivation and emotions; and gender and sexuality. Based in various historical traditions, the course is set in the context of contemporary psychological principles.

- PSY 230 – Theories of Personality: This course introduces the student to a number of personality theorists, their personalities, and their views in offering insight in to the question of the self. Psychoanalytic, social behavioral, traits, biological, humanistic, and cognitive are some of the theories that will be discussed in this course.

- PSY 240 – The Brain, the Body, and the Mind: This course provides an introduction to the investigation of physiological and neurological basis for human behavior. The student will be able to study and discuss various influences on personality development, such as pre-natal maternal behavior; gender; nature versus nurture; brain development; genetic composition; sensory motor interactions; learning disabilities; drug impacts; and neurological diseases.

- SCI 162 – Principles of Health & Wellness: This course reinforces the concept that learning effectively and living well involves both the mind and body. It presents the fundamentals of wellness and preventive health including strategic planning to attain and maintain personal optimal health. In addition, physical and mental diseases are discussed along with the dangers of environmental pollution, stress, addiction, and other negative factors that can affect personal health.

11/08 to present
Visiting Professor
DeVry University
Minneapolis, MN

PSY 110 – Principles of Psychology: This course provides a foundation for the understanding, prediction, and direction of behavior. Organized within a framework encompassing foundations, philosophy, general topics, and applications, the course provides an understanding of how psychological principles and concepts relate to professional and personal life. Topics include the scientific method, the biological basis of behavior, mental health, learning, motivation, personality, social influence, and group dynamics.

10/13 to 03/14
Adjunct Faculty
National Hispanic University
Oakland, CA

- PSY 315 – Psychological Disorders and Crime: This course focuses on the analysis of research findings, including research data from major studies, on psychological disorders and criminality in behavior, institution, community, and myth. Students evaluate contemporary theories about the relationship of psychological disorders and crime. Appropriate treatments, institutionalization, and detention or incarceration are explored.

- August 2007 to May 2014 - Adjunct Faculty, Southern Maine Community College, Portland, Maine

- CJU 115 – Introduction to Criminology: This course will define crime and evaluate the various ways crime is measured. Students will be provided with an overview of the more popular criminological theories, emphasizing the biological, psychological and sociological schools of thought. In addition, crime control and prevention strategies as they relate to each theory will be examined in terms of theory, practice and effectiveness.

- CJU 140 – Juvenile Justice: This course focuses on the development of the juvenile justice system and provides an overview of the administration of juvenile justice. Past and current theoretical approaches to delinquency will be discussed. Social, community, and environmental influences on delinquency will be covered to include; the impact of gender, family, peers, school, drug use and delinquency prevention. Public perceptions and punishment philosophies concerning juvenile crime will be explored. Topics of discussion will also include the police role in responding to juvenile crime and delinquency prevention. The Maine Juvenile Code will be covered as it governs the role of law enforcement, courts, and corrections.

- CJU 220 – Seminars in Criminal Justice: This course deals with underlying and current topics of policing in our society. The issues of police discretion, stereotyping, police candidate selection, paramilitary styles of police organization and operation, use of force, legal aspects of police administration, and policing the mentally ill are examples of the course's scope. Students will be challenged to examine values and beliefs they hold concerning the institution of law enforcement and the practice of policing as they currently exist.

- CJU 250 - Criminal Justice Internship: This course provides an opportunity for a student to work in the field of criminal justice. Students will spend a prescribed period of time working within a local criminal justice or public safety agency.

PROFESSIONAL BUSINESS EXPERIENCE

Summary:

- Approximately two years of experience facilitating psycho-educational groups and counseling of convicted adult male sex offenders for the Colorado Department of Corrections
- Licensed social worker conditional (10/14 – present)
- Managing and supervise instructors for the American Red Cross' Health & Safety program

PROFESSIONAL EXPERIENCE PORTFOLIO

09/14 to 01/15
Supervisor - Visitation Supervisors
Families United
Machias, ME

- Completed assessments on referrals for visitation services in compliance with agency policy
- Provided training and supervision to staff (six staff members) working in Family Visitation Center
- Participated in Child and Family Team and DHHS caseworker meetings to provide observation based data on visitation progress and issues
- Scored and tracked Adult/Adolescent Parenting Inventory (AAPI)
- Scheduled visitation services, reports, monitors, and manages program so that all performance measures required by DHHS are met and meets State and agency standards.
- Completed required reporting in an accurate and timely manner.
- Provided visitation services, as needed.

02/02 to 08/03
Sex Offender Treatment Therapist
Addicted Recovery Program, Inc.
Canon City, CO

- Evaluated inmate progress in Sex Offender Treatment & Monitoring Program (SOTMP), determined successful completion of mental health programs, certified progressive movement recommendations, and documented program progress.
- Assigned sex offender levels/needs and sexual violence codes to inmates to determine treatment needs, developed treatment plans, and assigned inmates to treatment programs.

- Facilitated intensive sex offender treatment to include development and implementation of treatment plans and conducted group therapy.
- Evaluated sex offenders under the supervision of an evaluator at the full operation level in order to make recommendations relating to an offender's risk to re-offend and amenability to treatment; recommend the level and intensity of offense-specific treatment needs; appropriateness and extent of community placement in which to perform a mental health sex offense-specific evaluation.
- Monitored inmates with mental health issues on a quarterly basis, made community referrals for inmates being released from the correctional system to other mental health organizations, and liaison between inmate and the parole officer surrounding their mental health issues.

01/98 to 05/01
Health & Safety Services Administrator
American Red Cross
Stuttgart, Germany

- Managed the Heather & Safety programs.
- Supervised over 509 instructor/instructor trainers.
- Maintained and processed all the Health & Safety Services records and reports per the national guidelines and policies.
- Ensured quality control procedures for training and certification procedures were met.
- Recruited and interviewed individuals for instructor/instructor trainer positions.
- Marketed the Health & Safety Services program to the military community in Germany.
- Organized and summarized data for monthly and annual reports.

EDUCATION

- 2012, Doctorate of Philosophy, Educational Psychology, Walden University
- 2004, Master of Science, Educational Psychology, Capella University

- 2000, Bachelor of Arts, Psychology with a minor in Sociology, University of Maryland

LICENSURE

- State of Maine: Department of Professional & Financial Regulations, Board of Social Worker Licensure #LSX15117 (LSW-C), Expires 10/31/16

COMMUNITY SERVICE

- Calais Little League Board Member-T-Ball and Minor League Coordinator and Softball Coordinator
- Perry Elementary School committee member
- Boys Scouts Cub Master

UNIVERSITY COMMITTEE SERVICE

- Fall/08 – Spring/2013, Advisor, Criminal Justice Program, Washington County Community College
- 2010 – 2012, Community Council Member, Adjunct Faculty Representative, Washington County Community College

RESIDENCIES

- 2009 – 2010, PhD Residency, Minneapolis, MN
- 2007, 2008, PhD Residency, Lansdowne, VA

RESEARCH INTERESTS

- Adult Education
- Criminology and Psychology
- Higher Education
- Online Learning
- Sense of Community
- Sex Offenders

Past Research: Research on traditional and non-traditional students in a rural community college focusing on online learning and sense of community.

Future Research: Online learning and sense of community among students at a university level.

PUBLICATIONS

Giero, P.A. (2016). *Perceptions Of Sense Of Community Of A Rural Community College.* Virginia Beach, VA: DBC Publishing.

Giero, P. A. (2012). *Perceptions of sense of community of a rural community college* (Order No. 3527382). ProQuest Dissertations & Theses. (1095102727). Retrieved from: http://search.proquest.com/docview/1095102727?accountid= 458

PROFESSIONAL MEMBERSHIPS

- American Psychological Association
- Society for the Teaching of Psychology (APA Div. 2)
- Educational Psychology (APA Div. 15)
- Association for Psychological Science
- Maine Psychological Association
- School Psychology (APA Div. 16)

HIGHLY COMPETENT SUBJECT AREAS

Technology: Computer proficient with expertise in MS Word, Excel, Outlook, and PowerPoint.

Learning Management Systems: eRacer, WebCT, BlackBoard, Canvas, e-Campus, and eCollege

Subject Matter Expert: Educational psychology, biopsychology, theories of personality, psychology and crime, foundations of psychology, developmental psychology, human relations, sociology, introduction to ethics, introduction to philosophy, speech courses, criminology, and juvenile justice

ABOUT THE AUTHOR

Dr. Patricia Giero, professor, facilitator, and psychotherapist, has worked in higher education since 2007. Giero's doctorate is in Psychology with an emphasis in Educational Psychology. She worked as a psychotherapist before becoming a community college professor in 2007.

She enjoys riding her Harley Davidson motorcycle, kayaking, swimming, and having fun with her three children as they watch the deer, moose, and pointy porcupine walk by her Maine coastal home.

ABOUT THE BOOK

This book is designed to provide knowledge of sense of community among traditional and nontraditional age students enrolled in online and traditional land-based learning environments.

There is a gap in the literature regarding sense of community for students in different learning environments of rural community colleges. The author established the process of examining a sense of community for students of rural colleges.

After reading the book, you will be able to take away information to be used to encourage course developers and online instructors to create and promote course activities that foster sense of community among students in online courses.

www.ingramcontent.com/pod-product-compliance
Lightning Source LLC
Chambersburg PA
CBHW062211270326
41930CB00009B/1706